THE CIVIL WAR IN WEST TEXAS AND NEW MEXICO

The Lost Letterbook of

Brigadier General Henry Hopkins Sibley

Edited and with an Introduction

by

John P. Wilson and Jerry Thompson

SOUTHWESTERN ⬖ STUDIES NO. 108

© 2001
Texas Western Press
The University of Texas at El Paso
El Paso, Texas 79968-0633

First Edition
ISBN 0-874-04283-6
PCN 2001090216

∞
Texas Western Press books are printed on acid-free paper, meeting
the guidelines for permanence and durability of the Committee on
Production Guidelines for Book Longevity of the Council on Library
Resources.

BRIGADIER GENERAL HENRY HOPKINS SIBLEY
(José Cisneros)

The Texas rebels and the Arizona cutthroats,
like the ancient Goths and Vandals, are at the very gates,
the portals of the Union, ready with battering cannons
to demolish the fairest fabric of freedom
ever devised by the wit of man.

W. M. Need to Simon Cameron
Fort Fauntleroy, New Mexico Territory
September 27, 1861

INTRODUCTION

Despite the relatively small number of men involved, one of the most important and fascinating campaigns of the Civil War was the ill–fated and grandiose 1861–1862 Confederate invasion of New Mexico Territory. The author of the New Mexico debacle was Brigadier General Henry Hopkins Sibley, a twenty–three–year veteran of the United States Second Dragoons. Sibley had served in New Mexico prior to the war, first at Cantonment Burgwin near Taos and later at Fort Union. A native of Louisiana, he resigned his commission in late May 1861 and set out for Richmond, Virginia. Traveling south into the Mesilla Valley, Sibley found ardent Southern sentiments ablaze. At Fort Bliss at Franklin (El Paso), Texas, he met with leading secessionists, and it was probably there, while waiting for the twice–a–week stage that would take him east through the twisting canyons and deserts of the Trans–Pecos to San Antonio, that Sibley's dream of conquering New Mexico for the Confederacy was conceived and refined.

In Richmond, Sibley met with the newly inaugurated president of the Confederate States of America, Jefferson Davis. The two men had much in common. Both were graduates of the United States Military Academy at West Point and had fought in the Mexican War. The two had become acquainted in 1855 and 1856 while Davis was serving as secretary of war in the Franklin Pierce administration, at which time Sibley was pushing for the adoption by the army of a conical–shaped tent he had conceived when stationed on the north Texas frontier in the winter of 1854–1855 while visiting a Comanche village.

Davis, who had extensive practical experience at the regimental level and a professional soldier's education, preferred seasoned West Point veterans such as Sibley. Moreover, Davis was impressed with Sibley's knowledge of the resources of New Mexico and the conditions of the Federal forces that continued to garrison the frontier forts in the distant territory. In the Confederate capital, Sibley gave Davis specifics as to the "quantity of government stores, supplies and transportation" in New Mexico.[1] Sibley convinced the Confederate president that he could recruit a brigade of enthusiastic Texans, equip them with arms taken from the Federal arsenals and forts in the Lone Star State, and easily seize New Mexico.

The New Mexico campaign would be self–sustaining, Sibley rationalized. An army of zealous Texas recruits could carry enough supplies until they reached Fort Bliss. From there Sibley would drive northward into the Mesilla Valley, where his men could sustain themselves. Facing a badly demoralized Federal force, Sibley was certain he could overrun or force the surrender of Fort Craig, the rock and adobe bastion in the south–central part of the territory. From there he would push his army up the Rio Grande, capture the supply depot at Albuquerque, raise the Stars and Bars over Santa Fe, and march on Fort Union, vital supply depot and the gateway to Colorado. His army swollen with "Southern men who were anxiously awaiting an opportunity to join the Confederate Army," Sibley would seize the gold and silver mines of Colorado.

The major objective of the campaign, as Sibley purportedly told one of his artillery officers, was the eventual conquest of California. "On to San Francisco" was to be the battle cry.[2] California, with its goldfields and vital harbors, would be a welcome addition to the Confederate States. In addition, negotiations would be opened with the adjacent Mexican states of Chihuahua and Sonora. An objective of Southern expansionists for two decades, these states, especially considering the chaotic political conditions existing in the Mexican republic at the time, could conceivably be acquired by negotiations or by conquest.[3]

A continental Confederate States of America stretching from Richmond to San Francisco might well speed diplomatic recognition by Great Britain and France, a vital component for the independence of the infant Southern republic. The diplomatic dividends from a successful campaign, despite the sacrifices required, might well make the campaign one of the most important of the war. Commissioned a brigadier general, Henry Hopkins Sibley would actualize a Confederate Manifest Destiny.

With orders to drive the Federal forces from New Mexico, General Sibley arrived in San Antonio to build his army of conquest at the same time that exciting news came out of the West.[4] Lieutenant Colonel John Robert Baylor, a dashing and daring Texan if there ever was one, had occupied the forts along the 652–mile San Antonio–El Paso Road. With 350 ragged and ill–equipped, yet determined Texans, he next struck north from Fort Bliss into the Mesilla Valley. Baylor seized the village of Mesilla, the largest settlement in the southern part of New Mexico, fought off a Federal attempt to drive him out, and although greatly outnumbered by the bulk of the Seventh United States Infantry, had forced by sheer intimidation the evacuation of Fort Fillmore. In an even more incredible maneuver, Baylor had captured the entire Fort Fillmore garrison as the soldiers fled through the Organ Mountains to the safety of Fort Stanton.[5] Baylor's amazing success was widely reported in the Texas press. With his ego ablaze, the fighting colonel was determined to eat his "Christmas dinner in Santa Fe" and boasted that "two hundred Texans could whip fifteen hundred Yankees anyday."[6] Baylor's achievements in New Mexico served to further convince Sibley of the ultimate success of his mission.

In the twentieth century, much time and effort was spent by scholars in reconstructing Sibley's New Mexico campaign. In particular, several historians studied the conduct and failure of the campaign from a Confederate perspective. In addition, biographies appeared on General Sibley and his adversary and friend, Colonel Edward Richard Sprigg Canby, as well as a number of subordinates on both sides.[7] Impressive studies detailed both the pivotal battles of Valverde and Glorieta.[8] Over thirty articles have described everything from whether the retreating Federals from Fort Fillmore had whiskey in their canteens in July 1861, as it was widely rumored at the time, to exactly who guided the "Pikes Peakers" in the destruction of the Confederate supply train in the depths of Apache Canyon during the Battle of Glorieta.[9] A number of diaries, journals, and memoirs from soldiers in both armies also appeared in print. Due to a continued proliferation of scholarship on the New Mexico campaign, primary sources with new revelations or details, as expected, dwindled to a trickle.

An exciting new discovery, however, is the letterbook of General Sibley. Sometime after the excruciating retreat of what remained of the beleaguered Army of New Mexico back to San Antonio in the summer of 1862, the letterbook came into the possession of Lieutenant Timothy Dargan Nettles, second in command of the Valverde Battery.[10] Nettles had first enrolled as a private in Captain John S. Shropshire's Company A of the Fifth Regiment of the T.M.V. at Columbus, Texas, on August 17, 1861. Nine days later he was mustered into Confederate service at San Antonio.[11] After being wounded at Glorieta, where he fought bravely, Nettles was promoted to first lieutenant in the newly created Valverde Battery on June 1, 1862.

After Captain Joseph D. Sayers, commander of the captured guns from Valverde and future governor of Texas, was wounded at the Battle of Fort Bisland in Louisiana in April 1863, Nettles was promoted to captain and given command of the battery, and he would serve bravely in that capacity for the remainder of the war. Returning to Texas, Nettles read medicine for a time, taught school, and tried farming five miles south of Buffalo, Texas, on a small tributary of Buffalo Creek.[12] All the time, Nettles kept in his possession Sibley's letterbook, even utilizing blank pages in the book to calculate farm income and expenses. When asked to write a history of the Valverde Battery, Nettles declined. "I have been requested time and again to write a history of the battery and have thought seriously of doing so," he told the *Seguin Anchor,* "but have decided (if I may say so) that a history would be an autobiographical sketch of myself during the war between the States, and I have no ambition to parade any of my soldier deeds."[13] Despite his reluctance to put in writing what would certainly have been a valuable set of recollections, we are grateful to Nettles for his preservation of Sibley's letterbook.

In addition to General Sibley, as many as 150 individuals are named in the letterbook. Most of these people are not well known, and, curiously enough, the only references to Jefferson Davis seem to be indirect ones: to His Excellency, the President.

Sibley held an independent command in the army but, in any event, would not have corresponded with President Davis. Instead he reported directly to General Samuel Cooper at Richmond. Cooper, with long service in the U.S. Army as a staff officer, resigned his commission on March 7, 1861, and then served the Confederate Army as its adjutant and inspector general throughout the war. Jefferson Davis appointed Leroy Pope Walker, a lawyer and legislator from Huntsville, Alabama, as his first secretary of war. Walker was inexperienced and failed lamentably at equipping the Southern armies, and he resigned on September 16, 1862, to be succeeded by Judah P. Benjamin. Benjamin continued in that office until February 18, 1862, when he became secretary of state.

Albert Sidney Johnston, colonel of the Second U.S. Cavalry from its formation in 1855, had been breveted a brigadier general in 1857. He penned his resignation at the end of May 1861 and passed through the Mesilla Valley and Texas on his way to Richmond, where Davis commissioned him a full general. Johnston died at the Battle of Shiloh on April 6, 1862. Josiah Gorgas, another career military man, served as chief of ordnance in the Confederate War Department. Lieutenant Colonel Abraham Myers was quartermaster general of the Confederate Army and Colonel Lucius B. Northrop held the post of commissary general until mid–February of 1865. Major Robert Hall Chilton, later a brigadier general, was part of General Cooper's staff in Richmond.

Luis Terrazas, one of Sibley's correspondents, was the influential governor of the state of Chihuahua. Within Texas, Sibley sought aid from Governor Edward Clark. Clark had succeeded Sam Houston on March 18, 1861, when Houston refused to take an oath of allegiance to the Confederacy. The election for governor that fall saw Francis R. Lubbock defeat Clark, who was then commissioned a colonel in the Confederate Army. Brigadier and later Major General Earl Van Dorn commanded the Department of Texas in 1861 and may have devised the strategy that led to Lieutenant Colonel John R. Baylor's occupation of the Mesilla Valley and capture of the U.S. garrison from Fort Fillmore in late July 1861. Van Dorn, like Governor Clark, seems to have given Sibley only limited support. After a reassignment in the East, Van Dorn returned to head the Trans–Mississippi District in 1862. He was shot and killed by a local doctor at Spring Hill, Tennessee, in 1863.

Colonel Henry E. McCulloch raised the First Texas Mounted Rifles and succeeded Van Dorn temporarily as head of the Department of Texas, until Brigadier General Paul O. Hébert assumed command on September 16, 1861. Hébert was shelved when Major General John B. Magruder took charge of the Trans–Mississippi Department in late 1862, under a revised system of command. In the summer and fall of 1861, Union commanders in New Mexico anticipated a second invasion from Texas led by Van Dorn, John R. Baylor, or Henry McCulloch, but this amounted only to a disinformation scheme. Clark, McCulloch, Hébert, and Magruder all survived the war. Brigadier General Hamilton P. Bee commanded a subdistrict of the Department of Texas on the lower Rio Grande. Major Edward F. Gray was Bee's adjutant, while Captain Charles M. Mason served as Van Dorn's adjutant officer.

A majority of the persons addressed or referred to in the letterbook belonged to the Fourth, Fifth, or Seventh Regiments, Texas Mounted Volunteers (the Sibley Brigade) or to Lieutenant Colonel Baylor's battalion of the Second Texas Mounted Volunteers and the Arizona volunteer companies attached to it. Most closely associated with the general were members of his own

Headquarters Field and Staff, beginning with his adjutant or A.A.G., Major Alexander M. Jackson, who actually wrote most of the letters. Jackson, a Mississippian appointed as secretary of New Mexico Territory in 1858, abandoned that post in 1861. He joined Sibley in San Antonio and served as his adjutant officer until November 1, 1862, resigning then to accept a post as chief justice of Arizona Territory.

Thomas P. Ochiltree, another Sibley loyalist, served as an aide–de–camp, which involved being acting adjutant general on occasion, bearer of dispatches, and general factotum. After the campaign, he became a staff officer for other prominent Confederate officers and later traveled to Europe to promote Texas interests. Sibley appointed Willis L. Robards as volunteer aide–de–camp and chief of ordnance until Robards resigned in May 1862. Despite the general's entire satisfaction with him, he never received a commission as an officer. Dr. Edward N. Covey was medical director of the Army of New Mexico and remained behind during the retreat, in charge of the Confederate hospital at Socorro, New Mexico. Other headquarters staff included Captain William Henry Harrison, the chief quartermaster who was absent most of the time in a vain effort to secure funding and supplies; Richard T. Brownrigg, chief commissary; and First Lieutenant Joseph E. Dwyer, another aide–de–camp who accompanied Colonel Reily to Chihuahua. Other staff officers were appointed but served only briefly or not at all.

When Sibley arrived at El Paso in December 1861 and proclaimed the Army of New Mexico, he incorporated Lieutenant Colonel John R. Baylor's battalion of the Second Texas Mounted Volunteers into this army and promoted Baylor to colonel. Baylor's subalterns included Major Edwin Waller Jr.; Captains Peter Hardeman, Charles L. Pyron, Isaac Stafford, Trevanion T. Teel (his artillery officer), and Bethel Coopwood; and Lieutenants William Simmons, Jesse Holden, and Michael Looscan. Because of casualties, promotions, and resignations, many changes in rank took place during the campaign. In June 1862, a former El Paso lawyer, Philemon T. Herbert, arrived from Richmond bearing a lieutenant colonel's commission and authority to raise what became the Arizona Battalion. The three companies in his battalion were Captain George Frazer's Arizona Rangers, Sherod Hunter's Company A, and Thomas Helm's Arizona Guards, all recruited locally and previously attached to Baylor's command. Herbert's Battalion of Arizona Cavalry was one of the last contingents to withdraw from Confederate Arizona. Joe Bowers, a private in Helm's company, escaped punishment for murder and transferred to the Arizona Rangers.

Colonel James Reily, another attorney and an early migrant to Texas, was absent from his Fourth Regiment, Texas Mounted Volunteers, on diplomatic missions to Chihuahua and Sonora during most of the New Mexico campaign. Lieutenant Colonel William Scurry commanded the regiment and proved more than capable, leading the Confederate forces at the Battle of Glorieta. His officers included Major Henry Raguet, Captain Henry Loebnitz, and Lieutenants James M. Noble, Henry G. Carter, and John Reily, the latter being the colonel's son.

Thomas Green, colonel of the Fifth Regiment, a former Texas Ranger and hero of the Texas Revolution, had served for twenty years as clerk of the Texas Supreme Court. Promoted to brigadier general in 1863, he was killed the next year leading an attack on Federal gunboats patrolling the Red River. In the Sibley Brigade, he was served by Lieutenant Colonel Henry C. McNeill; Majors Samuel Lockridge and John S. Shropshire, both killed in action; Captains Joseph Beck, Denman William Shannon, and Jerome McCown; Lieutenants Joseph D. Sayers, Marion B. Wyatt, William S. Wood, and Philip Fulcrod (the latter two commanded Green's artillery battery); and Chaplain Robert W. Peirce. Captain McCown, another former Texas Ranger, led the company of lancers that wisely did not charge at the Battle of Valverde, unlike the lancer company of Captain Willis L. Lang that was decimated. Captain McCown served as provost marshal in Mesilla at the end of the campaign.

Colonel William Steele's Seventh Regiment filled its ranks more slowly, and Lieutenant Colonel John S. Sutton led the first five companies to Fort Bliss the last week of January 1862. Steele himself and Major Arthur P. Bagby arrived a month later with three more companies and were too late to take part in the battles that spring. Captain Powhatan Jordan and Lieutenant (later Captain) Alfred Thurmond had accompanied Sutton, whereas Captains J. F. Battaile, William H. Cleaver, William L. Kirksey, and M. L. Ogden and the adjutant, Lieutenant Thomas Howard, all came with Steele. However, Captain Cleaver and five men were killed on July 1, 1862, during fighting with local Hispanics in the Mesilla Valley. Dr. George Cupples was the regimental surgeon while Dr. Henry Jacob Hunter was taken prisoner at Socorro along with Dr. Covey.

Not everyone with a military title actually held a commission. General Pelham, actually William Pelham, a former surveyor general of New Mexico Territory, left Santa Fe with Sibley on his retreat, but surrendered to the Federal commander when the Confederates camped opposite Polvadera. "Judge" Silas Hare (sometimes confused with Simeon Hart), also called Captain Hare, was living in Mesilla in 1861 when he led a hastily organized volunteer company to Fort Stanton and took charge of the abandoned government property there, holding it for the Confederates. He was appointed judge of the First District of Arizona Territory in October and held that office through May 1862, when he received appointment as a captain in the Arizona Brigade and served with it throughout the war. Captain John Phillips headed a group called the "Brigands," who were "employed" by Sibley's quartermaster department but never mustered into Confederate service.

Two of the most important civilians that appear in Sibley's letterbook are El Pasoans Simeon Hart and Josiah F. Crosby. Both were called "judge," since Hart had served as county judge and Crosby as district judge. Hart had settled at El Paso in 1849 and built a flour mill of modest size. In 1861 Sibley contracted with Crosby and Hart to purchase commissary supplies, but on his

arrival found that Baylor's men had consumed the available foodstuffs while Hart and Crosby had failed to amass adequate supplies from Mexico. Without hard money or "specie," the Mexicans
refused to sell anything. A campaign intended to be self–sufficient
faced hard times instead. The Richmond government commissioned Hart as a major and made him general purchasing agent
for the War Department in the Trans–Mississippi Department.
From 1863 he was especially active purchasing cotton for the Confederate Cotton Bureau. Crosby, originally a lawyer, became the
acting assistant quartermaster on Sibley's staff due to the absence
of Captain W. H. Harrison. Later he served nine months in
Europe, buying arms and munitions.

Not surprisingly, the letterbook rarely mentions Union offi-
cers. Colonel E. R. S. Canby headed the Federal forces in New
Mexico. Colonel Gabriel Paul, commanding the Fourth New
Mexico Infantry, had the dubious distinction of remaining at
Fort Craig during the Battle of Valverde and of holding Fort
Union at the time of the Battle of Glorieta. Lieutenant Colonel
Benjamin Wingate commanded Fort Craig in the late summer of
1861 and prevailed during the morning fighting at Valverde,
until ordered to withdraw. Colonel Nicolás Pino and Lieutenant
Colonel Jesús María Baca y Salazar surrendered the town of
Socorro with its garrison, the Second New Mexico Militia, to
Lieutenant Colonel Henry McNeill three days after the Confed-
erate victory at Valverde.

During the early months of the Confederate occupation, a San
Antonio entrepreneur, George H. Giddings, extended his San
Antonio and San Diego Mail Line westward all the way to Los
Angeles. By October the western terminus had shrunk to Mesilla,
but General Sibley rode a Giddings' stage into El Paso in Decem-
ber 1861 and rode one back again to San Antonio in July 1862.
One letter tells us that Giddings' agent in El Paso was a Mr.
Monigle. Not mentioned in his own memoirs and scarcely known
until now is that Giddings had a second line of business that was
even more important to Sibley: he was a Confederate agent for

procuring arms and munitions. In this, however, he appears to have had little success.

More information on most of the individuals named in the letterbook may be found in *The New Handbook of Texas* (1996), Martin H. Hall's *The Confederate Army of New Mexico* (1978), and a number of volumes about the Civil War in the Southwest. In his *Guide to the Archives of the Government of the Confederate States of America,* Henry P. Beers lists 191 Southern commanders, staff officers, and other persons whose wartime papers are available in various repositories.[14] With respect solely to the War Department Collection of Confederate Records (Record Group 109) at the National Archives, Beers tabulated 146 Confederate officers whose papers were donated or loaned for copying to the War Records Office during preparation of the *War of the Rebellion: Official Records* series.[15]

While not everyone whose documents survive is accounted for in this way, these names show what a tiny proportion of the thousands who served in the Confederate Army left little more than a service record. The 146 donors represented in Record Group 109 is almost the same as the number of officers (156) in the three regiments of the Sibley Brigade. If every one of Sibley's officers had contributed papers from their wartime service, this number would be greater than all donors or lenders represented in Record Group 109. Moreover, this total would be slightly more than three–quarters of the number of officers whose papers are found in all repositories. Another way to emphasize the low survival of personal papers is that only two of the 156 officers in Sibley's Brigade—Colonel William Steele and Assistant Surgeon John M. Bronough—were included in these lists. By any measure, the proportion of Confederate officers whose papers have come down to us is relatively small.

The Sibley letterbook is a major addition to this elite collection, and its value can be judged in several ways. Of the 147 individual letters the letterbook contains, only eight have been identified as having been published in the *Official Records,* Series I, Volumes 4 and 9. These eight—little more than 5 percent of the total—were printed from original letters (or contemporary copies) that survived. Their republication is not only of critical importance in the retelling of the Civil War in New Mexico Territory but serves to point out the erratic nature of the documents that made it into the *Official Records*. Of the eight, the letters of November 16 (or 17), 1861, and May 4, 1862, are the most significant, while the other six are equivalent in importance to those that adjoin them in the letterbook. Editors in the War Records Office published these eight letters and three others because these were probably all they found of Sibley's correspondence. We see now that Sibley, like Baylor and Canby, was fairly prolific as a correspondent, at least until the Army of New Mexico began its march toward Valverde.

Not all of the letters that Sibley wrote were copied into his letterbook. One missing letter was his February 22, 1862, report to Adjutant General Samuel Cooper on the Battle of Valverde.[16] Another was his March 31, 1862, letter to General Cooper on Glorieta, and a third one he addressed to Brigadier General Hamilton P. Bee on May 27, 1862.[17] The discrepancies in dates with several of the already published letters are additional evidence that his adjutant, the former secretary of the territory, Major Alexander Melvorne Jackson, either used the letterbook to draft the actual letters and sent "fair copies" to the recipients, or he copied letters in batches and not as they were written, missing a few in the process. This would explain how many documents were recorded out of chronological order and why some (as with those of February 22, March 31, and May 27, 1862) were overlooked entirely. A few pages had become detached in the original letterbook and appear to be missing, which explains why letters number 48 and 50 are incomplete.

What do Sibley's letters tell us that we did not know before about the Civil War in the Southwest? Primarily they demonstrate how he organized his small army, enlisted officers at the brigade and regimental levels, and sought to provide it with arms and equipment. In these respects, his correspondence is most enlightening, and if in the end he was judged a poor leader, he started off well enough.

The letterbook brings home in what a unique and difficult situation Sibley found himself. With a mandate from Jefferson Davis, he had almost a free hand to raise, equip, and provision a small army, then lead it across almost seven hundred miles of inhospitable Texas desert before reaching New Mexico. He received very little actual money for arms or supplies, although he could call on the governor of Texas and the officer commanding the Department of Texas for support and draw upon the credit of the government. Elsewhere, generals were assigned to commands, but Sibley had to create his own. His only responsibility lay with the adjutant general sixteen hundred miles to the east in Richmond.

These circumstances underlie Sibley's letters—sixty–one in all—before he even left San Antonio for New Mexico. The general evidently arrived in Texas with a certain number of blank commissions. After these had been utilized, he asked for confirmations by the adjutant general's office. This didn't work well, and his ordnance officer, Captain Willis L. Robards, actually served as a volunteer aide–de–camp until he finally resigned on May 5, 1862. The correspondence shows too that cooperation with the governor of Texas declined, as companies ordered to report to General Sibley had either disbanded, were too small for acceptance into Confederate service, or evidently chose to seek their glories elsewhere. This "misplaced reliance," as he called it, led Sibley to appeal directly to the public for recruits. More important, it threw his strategy off schedule, his original intention having been to invade New Mexico in the fall of 1861.

It is also evident that an inability to communicate with the commander of the Department of Texas left Sibley short of arms for his soldiers and artillery. He requested and requisitioned, but did not receive, badly needed supplies and munitions. In the end he had to buy whatever the local Confederate agent could find on the arms market or do without. If his somewhat understrength and poorly armed young Texans could have reached New Mexico in the fall of 1861, they might have prevailed. But by December, Baylor's men had eaten everything they had captured from the Union forces, plus whatever they had coerced from local citizens at El Paso and in the Mesilla Valley. Moreover, nobody in New Mexico, Chihuahua, or Sonora wanted to sell goods for Confederate currency.

The general summarized his difficulties succinctly in a letter of November 17, 1861, and while it probably sounded like whining back in Richmond, he had accomplished a great deal in the virtual absence of official support. The letterbook also shows how he selected his officers and how he sought to bring the men and their equipment and supplies together. He probably would have received little solace from knowing that the Union commander in New Mexico had similar problems, although by the fall of 1861, wagon trains loaded with provisions, munitions, and other supplies were rolling along the Santa Fe Trail into northern New Mexico from Fort Leavenworth, Kansas.

There are no accounts of battles in Sibley's letterbook. After the organization of his army and its movement to New Mexico, the letters concern administrative matters and operational considerations. What is absent, and agreeably so, is anything like the endless routine acknowledgments, cover letters, and references to court–martials, discipline, and personnel problems that typically fill most letterbooks of this era. Sibley's correspondence deals with matters of substance, even if some of the topics may be unfamiliar to scholars. Even on the less familiar subjects, there is new light on old mysteries.

For example, Sibley picked up a thread to the mysterious disappearance of a U.S. Army wagon train early in 1861. Reportedly the wagon master, one William Kirk, drove the train into Mexico and sold the wagons and contents for his private gain. Recent scholarship leaves unresolved whether the Knights of the Golden Circle, a secret, ardent states' rights, pro–Southern organization known to be active in San Antonio, or some other group of subversives engineered this disappearance.[18] From three letters written in early February 1862, Sibley indicated that he had Kirk and one other person under arrest and, in an amazing twist, offered to turn them over to the Federal commander at Fort Craig for possible prosecution. This never happened, largely due to the stubborn resistance of Colonel Tom Green, who commanded Sibley's Fifth Regiment of Mounted Volunteers, and Kirk went on to serve in the Confederate Army of New Mexico with an irregular group of ruffians called the "Brigands." Sibley thought that Kirk might have some $6,000 from the illegal sale on deposit at Franklin, Texas, but he conveniently omitted mention of this in writing to the Federal commander! If this money did exist, then Baylor and Sibley apparently never got their hands on it. And the disappearance of the wagon train evidently was a simple act of piracy by Kirk and a few associates; the Knights of the Golden Circle or the Confederate government or its agents had no hand in it.

Sibley also resolved what happened to a loyal citizen, John Lemon, after Baylor had him arrested, seized his property, and allowed or encouraged the hanging of an associate (Crittenden Marshall) in January 1862.[19] An inventory of Lemon's property included a number of weapons, harness, mules, and other valuable goods, including $1,741 in gold coin and $150 in gold dust.[20] Lemon apparently remained in custody until May, when Sibley ordered his release and the restoration of his property. This restoration would presumably have included his gold, if indeed Sibley was aware that gold coins and dust had been part of Lemon's goods.

Finally, Sibley seems to have brought to light the collaboration of a prominent Mesilla merchant, Thomas J. Bull, not previously known to have aided the South. He referred to a standing contract with Bull for all the flour his grist mill could produce, as well as a settlement of Bull's accounts for past supplies. Thomas Bull's evident reluctance to continue cooperation probably stemmed from his ten–month experience with Confederate supply officers and a well–founded expectation that he would be paid with worthless warrants or at best with Confederate script.

All of the above helps to illustrate the value of Sibley's letter-book in enabling us to understand better how he organized his brigade and sought to resolve innumerable problems prior to his invasion of New Mexico. The letters suggest that he was a much better administrator and diplomat than he was a military leader, but in the end it was his leadership in the field that really counted. He covered himself with excuses and alcohol, but only near the end of the campaign were his letters less than optimistic about his eventual success. He laid the withdrawal from Arizona (i.e., New Mexico) to want of supplies. Sibley told the government in Rich-mond what it wanted to hear, and Jefferson Davis can be excused for a letter of June 7, 1862, wherein he sent his far western com-mander his best wishes for continued success.[21]

Despite President Davis' congratulations, much of the blame for the failure of the campaign lay squarely on the shoulders of General Sibley. His biggest mistake was to have underestimated his enemy. He not only misjudged Southern sentiment in the Fed-eral Army in New Mexico, he miscalculated Union sentiments in California and Colorado. Sibley also displayed a great deal of igno-rance with respect to a proper understanding of the native Span-ish–speaking population of New Mexico, which was apathetic toward the South at best and decidedly Unionist at worst. He simi-larly failed to gauge the willingness and abilities of merchants in Chihuahua and Sonora to supply the Southern troops.[22] Sibley made a serious mistake in placing blind faith in the ability of his secessionist friends at El Paso, such as James Magoffin, Josiah F. Crosby, and Simeon Hart, in stockpiling badly needed foodstuffs and supplies at Fort Bliss.

In addition to the larger, more glaring strategic errors, numer-ous tactical mistakes can be blamed on Sibley. Sibley's regimental commanders made critical mistakes at Valverde and especially at Glorieta, many of which might have been avoided by a dynamic and assertive leader, in the Texas tradition, who was on the field of combat. General Sibley was absent during most of the Battle of Valverde and sixty miles to the rear during the pivotal Battle of

Glorieta. Surely from his excruciating and painful recollections of the march through South Pass, Wyoming, to Fort Bridger as a dragoon captain during the winter of 1857, and the ineffective 1860–1861 Navajo Expedition, he knew better than to advance deep into a hostile land in the dead of winter without a strong base of supply. All this had been emphasized time and again at West Point.

Major Trevanion T. Teel, Confederate artillery commander, perhaps put it best when he summarized Sibley's lack of leadership: "General Sibley was not a good administrative officer. He did not husband his resources, and was too prone to let the morrow take care of itself." This, plus the lack of "supplies, ammunition, discipline, and confidence," Teel thought, left little doubt that "failure was inevitable."[23] At the root of Sibley's lack of leadership and his failure during the campaign was his habitual drunkenness.

For twenty–three years, ever since he had taken his oath on the plain at West Point, Sibley had dreamed of commanding a great army in battle. When his one big moment in history arrived, he failed miserably. All his preconceptions about a conquest of New Mexico and the far West had been shattered. His romantic dreams of a Confederate empire in the Southwest had vanished. Had the New Mexico campaign succeeded, Sibley undeniably would have been hailed as one of the South's greatest military heroes, and the course of the Civil War might have been radically altered.[24] Instead, he had been badly defeated. As the last of his fatigued and sore–footed soldiers, many of them little more than scarecrows, limped into the streets of San Antonio in the summer of 1862, Confederate hopes for the realization of a western Manifest Destiny collapsed, never to be resurrected. Sibley's letterbook provides a rare glimpse into the Civil War in West Texas and New Mexico.

BRIGADIER GENERAL HENRY HOPKINS SIBLEY
(Arthur W. Bergeron Jr.)

"By geographical position, by similarity of institutions,
by commercial interests, and by future destinies,
New Mexico pertains to the Confederacy."

GENERAL H. H. SIBLEY
FORT BLISS, TEXAS
DECEMBER 20, 1861

". . . except for its political geographical position,
the Territory of New Mexico is not worth
a quarter of the blood and treasure
expended in its conquest."

H. H. SIBLEY TO S. COOPER
FORT BLISS, TEXAS
MAY 4, 1862

Brigadier General Henry Hopkins Sibley
(Library of Congress)

THE LETTERS

1.

New Orleans La.
July 10th 1861

Brig. Genl. E. Van Dorn
San Antonio Tex.
Genl:

I would suggest that the rendezvous of the
Brigade of Mounted Men mentioned in my letter to you of the 17th
by Lieut. McNeill, be at San Antonio, and that all organized
Companies presenting themselves be imediatly [*sic*] mustered into
the Service. I hope that this will meet with the approbation of Gov.
Clark and yourself.

Please order the Battery of artillery immediately.

I am Very respectfully
your obt Servt.
(Signed) H. H. Sibley
Brig. Genl. P.C.S.A.

2.

New Orleans La.
July 15th 1861

His Excellency
    Gov. E. Clark
    City of Austin
        Tex:
    Sir:

Lieut. H. C. McNeall [McNeill] C.S.A. will hand you this letter. Enclosed you will find a communication from Hon. L. P. Walker, Sec. of War of the Confederate States of America, directed to your Excellency, which with the information Lieut. McNeall is entrusted to communicate verbally to your Excellency will inform you of the purpose and general object desired.

Business of the utmost importance in regard to the expedition, which can only be accomplished in this City, will detain me here for several days; at the earliest day possible, I shall be in Austin, and communicate with your Excellency in person.

Lieut. McNeall is instructed to inform your Excellency of the whole object and intention of the movement in contemplation, and hope that you will extend every courtesy to him in your [unreadable] Excellency proceeds immediately to the organization of the forces specified, that Lt. McNeall will be placed in a position suitable to his high attainments as an officer, and his intimate knowledge (from long service) with the topography of the country and general disposition of the enemies forces. I commend him to you, Sir, as one every way qualified to occupy a field position in one of the Regiments.

I hope to have the pleasure of meeting you in a few days at Austin.

I have the honor to be
            Very respectfully
            your obt Servt
    (Signed)   H. H. Sibley
            Brig. Genl.
            P.C.S.A.

3.

New Orleans La.
July 15th 1861

Brig. Genl. E. Van Dorn
    Comdg. Dept. of Texas
        General:
                Lieut. H. C. McNeall C.S.A. will deliver you this
letter. Please find inclosed a communication from Adjt. Genl.
Cooper, C.S.A. addressed to yourself, which with the information
Lt. McNeall is intrusted to communicate to you, will inform you
of the object contemplated, & my desire, to obtain your valuable
co-operation in the same.

I commend Lt. McNeill to your especial consideration, &
desire that you will communicate fully with him upon all
particulars.

Business in regard to the success of the expedition and which
can only be attended to in New Orleans, requires my individual
attention for several days. I shall at the earliest practicable moment
leave for San Antonio, where I hope to arrive in a few days after
the receipt of this communication.

I desire particularly the assistance of Lt. McNeall in this affair,
he being a Texan possessing military qualifications of the highest
degree, thoroughly acquainted with the country &c. I hope His
Excellency Gov. Clark will place him in a position suitable to his
high qualifications.

                                    I am Sir very respect.
                                    your obt Servt
            (Signed)   H. H. Sibley
                        Brig. Genl. P.C.S.A.

4.

New Orleans La.
August 2nd 1861

General.

I have the honor to report to you that I shall leave the city tomorrow morning for Texas. I have been necessarily delayed here in consequence of the difficulty encountered by the disbursing officers assigned to my Command in procuring parties to go upon their bonds. Capt. Durfee has failed entirely here, and I have consequently ordered him to report to the War Dept. in Richmond Va., devolving the duties of his Department on the Quartermaster. Meanwhile I have dispatched all the other officers attached to my Staff to Texas, with all the communications addressed to the Governor and Genl. Van Dorn by the Sec. of War.

Success in the enterprise I have been charged with I regard as almost certain, but to ensure it, every element must be employed, hence the necessity of bringing every available influence to bear upon it. Guy Haden on duty in this city having been stationed many years in New Mexico, and having formed an extensive and most influential acquaintance is willing and most desirous of accompanying me. I would therefore earnestly request that his application to be permitted to serve in the capacity of one of the Field Officers be entertained favorably.

I have the honor to be
Very respectfully
Your obt Servt.

To
Genl. S. Cooper   (Signed)   H. H. Sibley
Adjt. & Insp. Genl. C.S.A.   Brig. Genl. P.C.S.A.

Genl. S. Cooper
Adjt. & Inspector Genl. C.S.A.
Richmond Va.

5.

San Antonio Texas
August 13th 1861

Official.

My Dear General.

In view of the turn of affairs in New Mexico, I deem it of the utmost importance to the success of my expedition, that the Santa Fe road west of Council Grove should be observed by a strong Cavalry force.

I would therefore suggest, that Col. McCulloch's entire Regiment, or as much of it as can be spared, be put in march northward for this purpose, with orders to communicate and co-operate with me, in the direction of New Mexico.

As the supplies reported to be en route for the Federal troops will be essential for the subsistence of my own forces, Col. McCulloch should be instructed in the event of his success, to hold them subject to my orders.

I am Genl.
with great respect
your Very obt Servt.

To Brig. Genl. Earl Van Dorn   (Signed)   H. H. Sibley
   Comdg. Dept. Texas   Brig. Genl. P.C.S.A.
     San Antonio Tex.

6.

Head Quarters Sibley's Brigade
San Antonio Texas
August 20th 1861

Sir.

You are hereby informed that you have been appointed
Colonel in the Second Regiment of Texas Volunteers, Sibley's
Brigade P.C.S.A., subject to the approval of the President.

If you accept, you will proceed to take the oath of office, before
some competent officer, authorized to administer oaths, and return
the same, with your letter of acceptance to me, at those Hd
Quarters.

		Very respectfully
To	(Signed)	H. H. Sibley
Thos. Green Esq.		Brig. Genl. P.C.S.A.
Austin Tex.		

You will repair without unnecessary delay to those Hd Quarters
and assist in the organization of your Regiment.

By order of Genl. Sibley
(Signed)   Tom P. Ochiltree
1st Lt. A.D.C. & Act. Ast. Adjt.

7.

H^d Qrs. Sibley's Brigade
San Antonio Tex. Aug. 20 [1861]

Sir.

You are hereby informed that you have been appointed Major
in the Second Regiment of Texas Volunteers, Sibley's Brigade,
Provisional Army of the Confederate States. Subject to the
approval of the President.

If you accept you will proceed to take the oath of office before
some competent officer authorized to administer oaths and return
the same, with your letter of acceptance to me at those Head
Quarters.

              (Signed)   H. H. Sibley

To   Brig. Genl. P.C.S.A.

Samuel A. Lockridge Esq.
   San Antonio Texas

8.

H^d Qrs. Sibley's Brigade
San Antonio Texas
Aug. 20th 1861

Sir:

You are hereby informed that you have been appointed Lt.
Col. in the Second Regiment of Texas Volunteers, Sibley's Brigade,
P.A.C.S. Subject to the approval of the President.

If you accept you will proceed to take the oath of office, before
some competent officer authorized to administer oaths, and to
return the same, with your letter of acceptance to me at those
Head Quarters.

              (Signed) H. H. Sibley

[no addressee, but   Brig. Genl. P.C.S.A.

intended recipient was   H^d Qrs. Sibley Brigade

Henry C. McNeill]

9.

Hᵈ Qrs. Sibley Brigade
San Antonio Texas
August 20, 1861

Sir.

You are hereby informed, that you have been appointed Colonel of the First Regiment of Texas Volunteers, Sibley's Brigade, P.C.S.A. Subject to the approval of the President.

If you accept, you will proceed to take the oath of office, before some competent officer authorized to administer oaths, and return the same, with your letter of acceptance to me at those Head Quarters.

(Signed)   H. H. Sibley
To   Brig. Genl. P.C.S.A.
Mr. Jas. Reily
    San Antonio Tex.

10.

Hᵈ Qrs. Sibley's Brigade
San Antonio Texas
August 20ᵗʰ 1861

Sir.

You are hereby informed that you have been appointed Asst. Com. of Subsistence, with the rank of Captain in Sibley's Brigade, P.C.S.A. Subject to the approval of the President.

If you accept, you will proceed to take the oath of office, before some competent officer authorized to administer oaths, and return the same with your letter of acceptance to me, at those Head Quarters.

To R. T. Brownrigg Esq.

Austin Texas

You will repair without delay to those Head Quarters, and enter on the discharge of your duties, in organizing your Department.

By order of Genl. Sibley
(Signed)   Tom P. Ochiltree
1ˢᵗ Lt. A.D.C. & A.A.A.G.

11.

H^d Qrs. Sibley Brigade
San Antonio Tex. Aug. 22/61

To His Ex. Gov. Clark
     Austin, Texas.
Sir.

I desire to call your attention to the tardiness, with which the Companys [Companies] designated by you, for my Brigade, are recruited. I am fearful that many of the enrolling officers will be unable to fill their Companies, in any reasonable length of time, yet will still retain their permission to recruit. I do not deem it necessary, to call your attention to the object of the expedition, and feel assured, that you will do everything in your power to facilitate its despatch. It is respectfully suggested, that all enrolling officers be required to have their companies organized by a certain day, if not that others will be appointed. I am in daily receipt of letters from gentlemen, all over the State tendering Companies, and with your Excellency's co-operation, I can organize my Brigade in the course of a few ~~days~~ weeks.

I enclose the names of gentlemen tendering Companies, with the request that they be ordered to rendezvous at this point with as little delay as possible. Those Companies have Companies fully organized and are only waiting for permission to march.

It is hoped that your Excellency's views may coincide with mine, as I feel and know how important for the success of the expedition, is your hearty co-operation.

I am Sir
Very respectfully
To   (Signed)   H. H. Sibley
Gov. E. Clark   Brig. Genl. P.C.S.A.
     Austin Texas

12.

Head Quarters Sibley's Brigade
San Antonio Texas Aug. 23rd 1861

Sir.

You are hereby informed, that you have been appointed Lt. Colonel in the First Regiment of Texas Volunteers, Sibley's Brigade, P.C.S.A. Subject to the approval of the President.

If you accept you will proceed to take the oath of office before some competent officer authorized to administer oaths, and return the same, with your letter of acceptance to me at those Head Quarters.

(Signed)   H. H. Sibley

To   Brig. Genl. P.C.S.A.
Wm. R. Scurry Esq.
   San Antonio Texas.

You will proceed without delay to those Hd Qrs. and assist in the organization of your Regiment.

By order of Brig. Genl. H. H. Sibley
Tom P. Ochiltree
1st Lieut. A.D.C. & A.A.A.G.

13.

San Antonio Tex:
August 23/61

Genl. S. Cooper
Adjt. & Inspec. Genl. C.S.A.
    Genl:
    I have the honor to request, that Mr. A. W. Jackson of
Gonzales Tex., late Sec. of the Territory of New Mexico, be
appointed Adjutant Genl. with the Brevet rank of Major with
orders to report to me for duty.

I have the honor to be
Very respectfully
your obt Servt.
(Signed)   H. H. Sibley
Brig. Genl. P.C.S.A.

14.

San Antonio Tex:
August 23rd 61

Genl. S. Cooper
    Adjt. & Inspector Genl.
        Genl.
    As the gentleman Mr. C. Durfee, whose name I handed to you
for the Com. of Subsistence for my Brigade, and whose
appointment was forwarded to him, through me, to New Orleans,
has failed to give the required bonds, and was therefore of no
service to me, I have the honor to present the name of Mr. Richard
T. Brownrigg of Austin, Texas for that appointment.

I have the honor to be
Very respectfully
your obt Servt.
(Signed)   H. H. Sibley
Brig. Genl. P.C.S.A.

15.

San Antonio Texas
August 23rd 61

Genl. S. Cooper
Adjt. & Inspector Genl. C.S.A.
Genl.

I have the honor to report to you, that I am progressing, but not as rapidly as I had hoped, in the organization of my Brigade.

The authority granted to Mrrs. [Messrs.] Terry and Lubbock to raise a Regiment of mounted troops for service in Virginia, has interfered materially with my success, as they seem to be drawing largely upon the organized companies I had counted upon. I trust however that I shall be enabled to commence the march in fifteen or twenty days. Every facility has been extended to me by Genl. Van Dorn, and a hearty co-operation by his Excellency Gov. Clark of Texas.

The recent signal and unexampled success of Lt. Col. Baylor 2nd Regiment T.M.R. in the capture of ten companies of Regulars (Infantry & Cavalry) and the successful establishment by him of a military Government over that part of New Mexico as Arizona [*sic*] will have relieved me of much work. My chief fear is, the disappointment to my troops in achieving a bloodless success. The destruction of property and stores (upon which I had mainly relied for the equipment and subsistence of my troops during the winter) by the demoralized Federal forces must be regarded as inevitable, and beyond my control.

As the companies constituting the Regiments of my Brigade, will be mustered into the Confederate States Service on the arrival of each at the general rendezvous (this city) the Field Officers must under the law be appointed by the President. Their names will be submitted to you in a few days and I trust the appointments will be issued accordingly at an early period.

I have the honor to be
Very respectfully your obt Servt.
(Signed)   H. H. Sibley
Brig. Genl. P.C.S.A.

16.

Head Quarters Sibley's Brigade
San Antonio Tex: Aug. 23rd 1861

Sir.

You are hereby informed, that you have been appointed Major in the First Regiment of Texas Volunteers Sibley's Brigade P.C.S.A. Subject to the approval of the President.

If you accept, you will proceed to take the oath of office, before some competent officer, authorized to administer oaths, and return the same, with your letter of acceptance to me at those Head Quarters.

(Signed)   H. H. Sibley
Brig. Genl. P.C.S.A.

To

H. W. Raguet Esq.

Nacogdoches Texas

You will proceed without unnecessary delay to those Head Quarters and assist in the organization of your Regiment.

By order of Brig. Genl. H. H. Sibley
(Signed)   Tom P. Ochiltree
1st Lt. A.D.C. & A.A.A.G.

17.

H^d Qrs. Sibley's Brigade
San Antonio Tex. Aug. 27/1861

Genl S. Cooper
    Adjt. & Inspector Genl. C.S.A.
        General.

I have the honor to report to you, that the Companies composing my Brigade are arriving at this "the rendezvous" daily. Genl. Van Dorn and his staff have been kindly extending to me every resource the Dept. affords in facilitating the organization. The Companies will be more or less deficient in arms. This defect we shall be enabled to remedy to some extent by purchase in the city, and by the use of lances. My chief embarrassment is to come, occasioned by the failure of the Staff Officers Quartermaster and Commissary "recommended by myself" to give the requisite bonds enabling them to draw funds. It is with a view to remedy this as promptly and as certainly as possible, that I dispatch my A.D.C. Lt. Tom P. Ochiltree with this communication.

As a remedy in the case of the Quartermaster Capt. Wm H. Harrison, I would suggest that some fit person in as [*sic*] near to Richmond, and who can give the necessary bonds be appointed, and the funds estimated for by Capt. Harrison be placed to his credit, or that the funds be intrusted to Lt. Ochiltree, with a blank appointment enclosed to me at this place, to be filled up by me with the name of some competent individual enabled to give the requisite bonds.

In the case of the Commissary, I have submitted the name of a gentleman Mr. R. T. Brownrigg of Texas for that appointment. He has sent forward the requisite bonds in anticipation. I recommend this gentleman especially to the favorable consideration of the Dept. In the meanwhile I have appointed him to perform the duties of this office.

I have assumed much responsibility in those matters, but I trust the President will hold me guiltless of too much presumption under the circumstances.

As the Troops constituting my Brigade are being mustered into the Service by Companies, and as it seemed to be the prevailing sentiment, both on the part of the Executive of the State and many influential citizens, that the appointment of Field Officers should rest with the President as provided for by law, and as the successful organization and drill of the Regiment admitted of no delay, I have made provisional appointments of the Field Officers, subject to the approval of the President. Those officers have been selected carefully from among the most able & influential citizens of the State, several of them having already attained fame in the Field, and in their selection I have had the assistance of His Excellency Gov. Clark, Genl. Van Dorn and other Gentlemen of influence and prominence in the State. I presume also that the Delegation in Congress from Texas, well know all the gentlemen mentioned. Their names are herewith submitted in a separate list.

The appointment of Mr. Alexander M. Jackson for Ass. Adjt. Genl. with the brevet rank of Major, I trust may be forwarded without delay. Besides having been the Sec. for the Territory of New Mexico, and hence especially qualified for the position, Mr. Jackson is a gentleman eminent in his profession and his selection I find is heartily approved by the people of the State.

By the advice of Genl. [Albert] Sidney Johnston, with whom I conferred freely on the subject, I have determined to avail myself of the authority given me in my instructions and take a larger force than I had first intended "say three thousand men." A Compy. of Volunteer Artillery fully equipped, having offered their services, I have accepted it, and at the instance of Genl. Van Dorn I have dispensed with the Company of Regulars "First Cavalry" I was authorized to take.

I shall also avail myself if I find it to the interest of the Government of the service of one or more of the resigned officers expected here daily from California. This I trust will meet with approval of the Department.

I am Sir

Very respectfully
your obt Servt.

(Signed)   H. H. Sibley
Brig. Genl P.C.S.A.

"Act. Ass. Adjt. Genl. A. M. Jackson Aug. 19/61"
Act. Com. Sub: R. T. Brownrigg Aug. 19/61.

List of appointments made by Brig. Genl. H. H. Sibley P.C.S.A. Subject to the approval of the President.

1st Regiment T.M.V. Sibley's Brigade

James Reily	Colonel	August 19th 1861
Wm P. Scurry	Lt. Col.	" 23, 1861
H. W. Raguet	Major	" 23, 1861

2nd Regiment

Thomas Green	Colonel	August 20th 61
Henry C. McNeill	Lt. Col.	" " "
Saml. A. Lockridge	Major	" " "

18.

H^d Qrs. Sibley's Brigade
San Antonio Tex. Aug. 28th 1861

Ass. Adjt. Genl.
    Dept. of Texas
        Sir.

I have the honor herewith to forward the names of the following officers appointed in the Staff and Field, in my Brigade, viz:

James Reily	Col.	1st Regt.
Wm P. Scurry	Lt. Col.	" "
H. W. Raguet	Major	" "
Thos. Green	Col.	2nd Regt.
H. C. McNeil[l]	Lt. Col.	" "
S. A. Lockridge	Major	" "
A. M. Jackson	Act. Ass. Adjt. Genl.	
Henry Beaumont	Act. Quartermaster	

Respectfully

To Ass. Adjt. Genl.
Dept. of Texas
           your obt Servt.

Act. Ass. Adjt. Genl.

19.

H^d Qrs. Sibley Brigade
San Antonio Tex. Aug. 29/61

His Ex. Gov. Clark
    Gov. of State of Texas
    Sir:
    I am directed by Genl. Sibley to enclose to you for
acceptance or rejection the within application of Mr. H. W. Cook,
and to request that you will advise that gentleman of your
action.

		With high respect
		your obt Servt.
To Gov. E. Clark	(Signed)	A. M. Jackson
Austin Texas		Act. Ass. Adjt. Genl.

20.

H^d Qrs. Sibley Brig.
San Antonio Texas
August 31st 1861

Mr. Geo. H. Giddings
    San Antonio
            Sir:
    As the troops constituting my Brigade, in consequence of the
great drain on the State for [sic] other quarters, will be more or less
deficient in Arms—I have to request you "as the agent of the
Government" to secure for the troops under my command all the
available arms possible, on the most reasonable terms.

		I am Sir very respectfully
To		your obt Servt.
G. H. Giddings Esq.	(Signed)	H. H. Sibley
San Antonio Tex.		Brig. Genl. P.C.S.A.

21.

H^d Qrs. Sibley Brigade
San Antonio Texas.
Sept. 2nd 1861

To
Adjt. Genl.
    S. Cooper
General.

I observe in the newspapers a statement to the effect that the U.S. Government has ordered Genl. Sumner to organize in California a force of from five to ten thousand men, for the purposed occupation of New Mexico. Gov. Clark of this State placing some reliance on this statement, offers me the service of four Regiments of State troops which he expects to have upon the northern frontier of the State within some two or three weeks. Having no means, however, of estimating the degree of credit to be given to the statement, or the probability that any additional force will be thrown by the enemy into that territory, I am not disposed to accept these re-enforcements without authority to that effect from the superior authority at Richmond, who must have means of information in regard to the probability of the emergency arising, who are inaccessible to me.

I beg therefore to be placed, at as early a day as possible, in possession of the views or orders of the Dept. in regard to the offer of Gov. Clark, and if I am directed to accept it, whether the Troops, so placed under my command, shall be mustered into the service of the Conf. States, or only employed as a co-operative force in the service of the State. In regard to this latter point, Gov. Clark has not indicated to me any preference or expectation.

		I am General
To		Very respectfully
Genl. S. Cooper		your obt Servt.
Adjt. & Insp. Genl. C.S.A.	(Signed)	H. H. Sibley
Richmond Va.		Brig. Genl. P.C.S.A.

22.

H^d Qrs. Sibley's Brigade
San Antonio Tex. Sept. 6th [1861]

R. B. Lambane 1st Lt.
    or S. F. Noble 2nd Lieut.
        Ringgold Barracks Texas
Gentlemen.

Your favor of August 29th to Genl. H. H. Sibley, offering him the services of the Company referred to by you, is received.

I am instructed by the Genl. to reply that he will be gratified to have the services of your Company, but at the same time, to advise you that it will be out of his power to furnish arms and equipments for it. In fact they are not here to be had. The General hopes, however, that your Company will be able to arm and equip itself and to report at an early day. I may add uniformity in the arms or equipments is not expected. So that they are serviceable and efficient, is all that is required.

Very respectfully
your obt Servt.
(Signed)   A. M. Jackson
Act. Ass. Adjt. Genl.

23.

H^d Quarters Sibley Brigade
San Antonio Tex. Sept. 6th 61

Clark L. Owen Esq.
    Texana
        Texas

Sir.

    Your favor relative to Capt. Rick, addressed to Genl. Sibley, has been received, and in reply I am directed by the Genl. to say that if Capt. R. shall be able to raise a Company, mounted, armed and equipped, the General will be gratified to accept their services. There is no position however of a supernumery [*sic*] Captain or other Commissioned Officer, to which as you seem to suppose the Genl. could appoint Capt. R. The organization of the different corps is prescribed by law, and beyond the offices so created there are none to be filled.

                                  Very respectfully
                                  your obt Servt.

C. L. Owen Esq.   (Signed)   A. M. Jackson
    Texana   A.A.A.G.
        Texas

24.

H^d Qrs. Sibley Brigade
San Antonio Tex. Sept. 6th [1861]

Mr. J. D. Sayers Esq.

Sir:

You are hereby informed that you have been appointed First
Lieut. in the Second Regiment of this Brigade. If you accept you
will forthwith take the oath of office and file the same together
with your letter of acceptance in the office of the Adjutant General
of this Command, and thereupon report for duty as Adjutant of
same Regiment to Col. Thos. Green Commanding the same.

Very respectfully
(Signed)   A. M. Jackson

J. D. Sayers Esq.   Act. Ass. Adjt. Genl.
San Antonio Tex.

25.

Austin Texas
Sept. 8th 1861

His Excellency

Gov. Edward Clark

Sir:

After mature consideration, your offer to place two Regiments
of State Cavalry at my disposal, for service in the direction of Fort
Union, New Mexico, to co-operate with other forces I am to lead
in person in the same direction, I have the honor to inform you
that the proposition is accepted and that I shall depend upon their
services accordingly.

I have the honor to be
Very respectfully
your obt Servt.

To
Gov. E. Clark   (Signed)   H. H. Sibley
Austin Texas   Brig. Genl.

26.

H^d Qrs Sibley Brigade
San Antonio Tex. Sept. 14 [1861]

Rev. R. W. Pearce [Peirce]
Sir.

I have the honor to inform you that, on the recommendation of the Council of Administration, you have been appointed Chaplain, in the Second Regiment, Sibley Brigade, subject to the approval of the President.

If you accept, please forward your letter of acceptance, and report in person at this office.

I am Sir
Very respectfully
your obt Servt.

Rev. R. W. Pearce   (Signed)   A. M. Jackson
    San Antonio Tex.   Act. Ass. Adjt. Genl.

27.

H^d Qrs. Sibley Brigade
San Antonio Texas
Sept 15th 1861

Captain.

The General Com^{dg} directs that you will proceed at once to the eastern counties of this State, and assist in organizing with as little delay as possible two or more Companies, "not exceeding five of Cavalry, fully armed and equipped" for this Brigade.

Should you be successful within twenty days, and the main Column has marched from this point, you will follow as rapidly as possible.

Very respectfully
your obt Servt.

Capt. D. W. Shannon   (Signed)   A. M. Jackson
    San Antonio Tex.   Act. Ass. Adjt. Genl.

28.

H^d Qrs. Sibley Brigade
San Antonio Tex. Sept. 16 [1861]

Genl. S. Cooper
Adjt. & Inspector Genl. C.S.A.
Richmond Va.

Sir:

I have the honor to report that I have appointed Joseph D. Sayers a First Lieutenant in the Provisional Army of the Confederate States, subject to the approval of the President, and assigned him to duty as Adjutant of the Second Regiment of this Brigade.

This appointment was made on the urgent application of Col. Green, Com^{dg} said Regiment, who represented to me, that there was among the Lieut's of the Companies, none in the least degree conversant with the duties of the Adjutant. Mr. Sayers is a graduate of the Bastrop Military Academy, an Institute held in high esteem in this State, and is a young man, as I am assured by Col. Green and many others, finely qualified for the position assigned him.

In view of those circumstances and the interest of the service, I hope my action herein will be approved, and that the commission for Mr. Sayers, to date from the 6th instant, will be forwarded at an early date.

I am Genl.
Very respectfully

To   your obt Servt.

Genl. S. Cooper   (Signed)   H. H. Sibley

    Adjt. & Insp. Genl. C.S.A.   Brig. Genl. P.C.S.A.

    Richmond Va.

29.

Hᵈ Qrs. Sibley Brigade
San Antonio Tex. Sept. 21 [1861]

Major S. Macklin
    A.Q.M., C.S.A. San Antonio
Major.

I am instructed by General Sibley to apprize you of the urgent necessity of the troops under his command for the means of placing their fire arms in a serviceable condition.

Desiring to avoid troubling the Dept. here with this matter, the General directed the A.Q.M. of this Brigade to hire smiths and implements to make the repairs necessary. The A.Q.M. of the Brigade, however, after using his best exertions to carry out those directions, has failed to procure the necessary mechanics and tools for the purpose.

Under those circumstances, and in view of the absolute necessity of putting the arms in a condition of efficiency, I am instructed by the General to apply to you, as a last resort, for such assistance, as it may be in your power to afford, by furnishing the workmen, shops &c, to perform those repairs.

                              Very respectfully
                              your obt Servt.
Maj. S. Macklin   (Signed)   A. M. Jackson
Qr. Master Dept. Texas   Act. Ass. Adjt. Genl.
San Antonio Tex.

30.

Hd. Qrs. Sibley Brigade
San Antonio Texas
September 22nd 1861

Col. J. Reily & Lt. Col. H. C. McNeill
    Comdg Regts. Sibley Brigade
        Sir.

I am directed by Genl. Sibley to inform you that it is his purpose to organize for service with each Regiment of this Brigade, a Corps of Field Artillery to consist of four small Howitzers to be officered and manned by details from the Regiments to which they are attached.

Accordingly, you will cause to be detailed from your Regiment for this service one First Lieut., one Second Lieut., two Sergeants, two Corporals, and thirty Privates. Such details to be specially selected with a view to the proposed service.

It is intended that the Horses of the men detailed for this purpose shall be used for the draught and service of the Batteries.

Very respectfully
    your obt Servt.
(Signed)   A. M. Jackson
        Act. Ass. Adjt. Gen.

31.

Hd. Qrs. Sibley Brigade
San Antonio Tex. Sept. 28, 61

To His Excellency
    Edward Clark
        Governor of State of Texas
Sir:

By direction of Brig. Genl. Sibley, I inclose you the within account, presented to him for payment, for the purpose of ascertaining whether it is just and should be paid by the C.S. The general received under your frank, the map referred to in the account and supposed that you had caused it to be prepared in some of the public offices of the State, and that consequently it was not properly a subject of charge by an individual.

It is respectfully requested, therefore, that your Excellency will verify or correct this understanding of the General, with a view of enabling him to make a just disposition of the demand.

                  I have the honor to be
                  your Ex. obt. Servt.
To   (Signed)   A. M. Jackson
Gov. E. Clark   A.A.A.G. C.S.A.
Austin Texas

32.

Hd. Qrs. Sibley Brig.
San Antonio Texas
September 30th 1861

Lieut. Arthur Shaaff
San Antonio Texas
Sir:

By direction of Brig. Genl. H. H. Sibley C.S.A. Com^{dg} this Brigade I enclose you the within appointment as Captain in the Provisional Army of the Confederate States.

If you accept, you will please take the prescribed oath of office, and return the same to this office, together with your letter of acceptance.

Very respectfully
your obt. Servt.

Lt. A. Shaaff   (Signed)   A. M. Jackson
San Antonio Tex.   Act. Ass. Adjt. Genl.

33.

Hd. Qrs. Sibley Brigade
San Antonio Texas
September 30th 1861

Genl. S. Cooper
     Adjt. & Inspector Genl. C.S.A.
Sir.

I have the honor to communicate that under the authority conferred upon me by the President, for the efficient organization of this Brigade, I have this day appointed Lieut. Arthur Shaaff, late 1st Lieut. in the regular service of the Confederate States, to be Captain in the Provisional Army, subject to the approval of his Excellency the President.

This appointment has been made to provide for the urgent necessity for an Ordnance Officer to this Command, to which duty Captain Shaaff will be assigned. The military experience and professional knowledge, so important in this position, was not to be found in any of the officers belonging to the Brigade, so that it could not be efficiently filled by detail.

Under those circumstances I hope the appointment will be ratified by his Excellency, in which event I request that his Commission (to bear date from this day) be forwarded to the care of the Commanding Officer of this Dept.

		I am General
To		Very respectfully
Genl. S. Cooper		your obt. Servt.
Adjt. & Insp. Genl. C.S.A.	(Signed)	H. H. Sibley
Richmond Va.		Brig. Genl. C.S.A.

34.

Hd. Qrs. Sibley Brigade
San Antonio Oct. 3rd 1861

1st Lieut. & Adjt.
 J. D. Sayers
  2nd Regt. of Sibley Brigade
Sir:
 You will proceed to muster into the service Captain P. Jordan's
Company, with such men as may be presented for that purpose.

        By order of Genl. Sibley
        yours &c
Lt. J. D. Sayers   (Signed) A. M. Jackson
San Antonio Tex.   A.A.A.G.

35.

Hd. Qrs. Sibley Brigade
San Antonio Texas
October 4th 1861

Captain Wm Steele
 San Antonio Texas
Sir.
 By direction of Brig. Genl. H. H. Sibley C.S.A. Comdg this
Brigade I enclose you the within appointment as Colonel of the
Third Regiment of this Brigade, Provisional Army of the
Confederate States.
 If you accept, you will please take the prescribed oath of office,
and return the same to this office, together with your letter of
acceptance.

        Very respectfully
        your obt Servt.
Col. Wm Steele   (Signed) A. M. Jackson
San Antonio Tex.   Act. Ass. Adjt. Genl.

36.

Hd. Qrs. Sibley Brig.
San Antonio Texas
October 4th 61

Genl. S. Cooper
Adjt. & Insp. Genl. C.S.A.
Richmond Va.
General.

I have the honor to report that I have appointed Captain William Steele, late Capt. 2nd Drags. U.S.A. to be Colonel of the Third Regt. of this Brigade, P.A.C.S. Subject to the approval of the President.

If this appointment is confirmed by his Excellency, I request that Col. Steele's Commission (to date from this day) be forwarded to the care of the Commanding Officer of this Department.

		I am, General
		Very respectfully
Genl. S. Cooper		your obt Servt.
Adjt. & Insp. Genl. C.S.A.	(Signed)	H. H. Sibley
Richmond Va.		Brig. Genl.

37.

Hd. Qrs. Sibley Brigade A.G.O.
San Antonio Texas Oct. 8th 61

Col. James Reily
  Com^{dg} 1st Regt.
Sir:

By direction of the General Com^{dg} I communicate to you his desire that you prepare your Regiment for the march with as little delay as possible. Your attention is particularly directed to seeing that the proper kinds and quantities of Ordnance stores are obtained for your Command, and indeed every thing necessary to put it in a state of efficiency for active operation.

You will report the earliest day your Regiment shall be ready to advance.

<table>
<tr><td></td><td></td><td>Very respectfully
Your obt Servt.</td></tr>
<tr><td>Col. J. Reily</td><td>(Signed)</td><td>A. M. Jackson</td></tr>
<tr><td>Com^{dg} 4th Regt.</td><td></td><td>Ass. Adjt. Genl.</td></tr>
<tr><td>San Antonio Tex.</td><td></td><td></td></tr>
</table>

38.

H^{d} Qrs. Sibley Brigade A.G.O.
San Antonio Tex. Oct. 8th 61

Captain.

The General Com^{dg} directs that with as little delay as possible, you will ascertain from the Ordnance Officer of this Dept., and report to those Head Quarters, what supply of ammunition of all kinds both for Howitzers and small arms, can be furnished to this command.

<table>
<tr><td></td><td></td><td>I am Captain
your obt Servt.</td></tr>
<tr><td>Capt. A. Shaaff</td><td>(Signed)</td><td>A. M. Jackson</td></tr>
<tr><td>O.O. S.A. Texas</td><td></td><td>Act. G.</td></tr>
</table>

39.

Hd. Qrs. Sibley Brigade A.G.O.
San Antonio Tex. Oct. 8th 1861

Mr. J. S. Sutton Esq.

Sir.

I have the honor to enclose you an appointment by Genl. H. H. Sibley Com^{dg} this Brigade to be Lieut. Colonel of the Third Regiment of this Brigade. Subject to the approval of the President of the Confederate States.

If you accept you will please take the oath of office prescribed by law and file the same in this office together with your letter of acceptance.

		Very respectfully
		your obt Servt.
J. S. Sutton Esq.	(Signed)	A. M. Jackson
San Ant: Tex.		A.A.G.

40.

Hd. Qrs. Sibley Brigade A.G.O.
San Antonio Texas Oct.8th 61

Genl. S. Cooper

Adjt. & Inspector Genl. C.S.A.

General.

I have the honor to report, that I have appointed Mr. J. S. Sutton Lieut. Colonel of the Third Regiment of this Brigade, Provisional Army of the Confederate States. Subject to the approval of the President.

If this appointment is confirmed by his Excellency, I request that Lieut. Col. Sutton's Commission be forwarded to the care of the Commanding Officer of this Department.

		I have the honor to be
		Very respectfully
Genl. S. Cooper		your obt Servt.
A.& I.G. C.S.A.	Signed)	H. H. Sibley
Richmond Va.		Brig. Genl.

41.

Hd. Qrs. Sibley Brigade A.G.O.
San Antonio Tex. Oct. 9th 61

Mr. Thos. C. Howard Esq.
    San Antonio Tex.
Sir:

I have the honor to enclose you an appointment by Genl. H. H. Sibley Com^{dg} this Brigade, to be Adjutant of the Third Regiment of this Brigade. Subject to the approval of the President.

If you accept, you will please take the oath of office, prescribed by law, and file the same in this office together with your letter of acceptance.

Very respectfully
your obt Servt.

T. C. Howard Esq.   (Signed)   A. M. Jackson
San Antonio Tex.
    Act. G.

42.

Hd. Qrs. Sibley Brig: A.G.O.
San Antonio Tex. Oct. 9th 61

Capt. A. Shaaff
Ordnance Officer
Captain:

Your report of this date has been laid before the General Com^dg, who directs me to instruct you to receive from the Ordnance Officer of this Department all of the ammunition, which it can spare for the service of this Command, comprising all the various kinds requisite for large and small arms of all description.

There being but little probability of procuring any additional supply after this Command shall move forward, it is very important that a full supply should be obtained here.

I am Captain
your obt Servt.
(Signed)   A. M. Jackson
Ass. Adjt. Genl.

43.

Hd. Qrs. Sibley Brigade A.G.O.
San Antonio Texas Oct. 9th 61

Genl. S. Cooper
Adjt. & Inspector Genl. C.S.A.
General.

I have the honor to report that I have appointed Thomas C. Howard Adjutant of the Third Regiment of this Brigade, with the rank of First Lieutenant Provisional Army of the Confederate States. Subject to the approval of the President.

If this appointment is confirmed by his Excellency, I request that Adjutant Howard's Commission be forwarded to the care of the Commanding Officer of this Department.

(Signed)   H. H. Sibley

Genl. S. Cooper   Brig. Genl.
A. & I.G. C.S.A.

44.

Hd. Qrs. Sibley Brig. A.G.O.
San Antonio Tex. Oct. 12th 61

Genl. S. Cooper
Adjt. and Insp. Genl. C.S.A.
Genl.

I have the honor to enclose the resignation of Captain [John F. F.] Doherty of the 1st Regt. of this Brigade, tendered by him on account of ill health.

I have accepted this tender, subject to the approval of the President, and have ordered an election forthwith to fill his vacancy.

In view of the urgent necessity of an immediate and efficient organization of this command, I hope this action will be approved.

I have the honor to be
Very respectfully

Genl. S. Cooper   your obt Servt.
A.& I.G. C.S.A.   (Signed)   H. H. Sibley
Richmond Va.   Brig. Genl.

45.

Hd. Qrs. Sibley Brigade
San Antonio Tex. Oct. 12th 61

Col.

I have the honor to suggest the imperative necessity which exists of forwarding the funds estimated for by my Brigade Commissary, by Capt. W. H. Harrison Q.M. to the Brigade, who visits Richmond if necessary especially to obtain them unless they can be forwarded to New Orleans to his order.

My Commissariat must be supplied with funds, or the efficiency of this Brigade will be weakened.

Captain Harrison bears Maj. Brownrigg's letter of acceptance [of] his bonds and authority to receive the funds belonging to his Department.

I am Very respectfully
your obt Servt.

To   (Signed)   H. H. Sibley
Col. L. B. Northrop   Brig. Genl.
   Com. Genl.

46.

Hd. Qrs. Sibley Brigade A.G.O.
San Antonio Tex: Oct. 12th 1861

Mr. A. P. Bagby
San Antonio Texas
Sir:

l have the honor to enclose you an appointment by Genl. H. H. Sibley Com^dg this Brigade, to be Major of the Third Regiment of this Brigade. Subject to the approval of the President.

If you accept, you will please take the oath of office prescribed by law, and file the same in this office, together with your letter of acceptance.

Very respectfully
your obt Servt.

A. P. Bagby Esq.   (Signed)   A. M. Jackson
San Antonio Tex.   Ass. Adjt. Genl.

47.

Hd. Qrs. Sibley Brigade A.G.O.
San Antonio Tex: Oct. 18th 61

His Excellency
Edward Clark
Governor of the State of Texas
Sir:

I have the honor to enclose for your information a copy of a communication this day received by the Genl. Com^dg this Brigade from the Adjt. & Insp. General of the C.S. relative to the acceptance of additional Regiments.

I have the honor Sir to be
your obt Servt.

Gov. E. Clark   (Signed)   A. M. Jackson
Austin Tex.   Ass. Adjt. Genl.

48.

[incomplete; initial part of letter missing]

tofore given you the Genl. Commanding desires me to say that you will immediately on your arrival at Fort Bliss have an accurate inventory of all the arms, and ammunition there taken, and that you will have them secured for the Regiments to follow, as upon this supply much reliance is placed for the completion of their armament.

Col. J. Reily   [no signature block]
Comdg 4th Regt.

49.

Hd. Qrs. Sibley Brigade
San Antonio Tex. Oct. 22/61

Col.

You will receive orders of this date to take up the line of march with your Regiment tomorrow in the direction of El Paso.

The General Com^{dg} deems it expedient to indicate to you officially the purpose of the Campaign upon which this Command is about to enter and his views in regard to the same, so far as they may affect your Corps and duties. In the language of the Government at Richmond, the General is entrusted with the important duty of driving the Federal Troops from the Department (New Mexico) at the same time securing all their arms, supplies and materials of War.

Commanding the advanced force of this command your chief exertions will of course be directed to the objects thus prescribed.

On arriving at El Paso (should you do so before the arrival of the General) you are authorized to assume the Command of all the forces of the Confederate States within the district of country known as Arizona and also at Fort Bliss or between there and the frontier of Arizona. So much depends upon the condition of affairs which you shall find to exist there and in the adjacent country occupied by the enemies Troops, and upon the condition of your own force upon your arrival there, that the General leaves you entirely untrammeled by instructions in regard to assuming offensive operations before he shall arrive. Should an advance be advisable in your judgement you will not hesitate to make it and to resort to every resource known to civilized warfare to sustain it. Should you deem an advance inadvisable until reinforcements are received you will make such dispositions of your forces as your own judgement shall direct.

For the supply of your troops both in the Qr. Master and Commissary department you are empowered fully to provide in such manner as shall be deemed most expedient whether by concluding contracts for the delivery of such supplies or for their purchase in open market. Liabilities thus incurred by you or by your authority will be provided for by Drafts on New Orleans, drawn by the Brigade officers charged with those Departments or by any other means at their command which may be preferred.

You are also authorized and it is desired that you should procure in the same manner as large a supply of forage as possible for the use of the whole Brigade to be delivered and kept at such points as you shall designate. It is also very desirable you should if possible procure in the same way munitions of War adapted to the arms with which this Command is equipped. Ammunition of all kinds both for the field Batteries and the small arms. Any loans which you may be enabled to effect from patriotic persons to enable you to carry out those objects will be sacredly observed and provided for.

It is the desire of the General that while en route as well as after your arrival in Arizona you should furnish to all Citizens of the Confederate States and of that Territory and their property, such protection as you can against the hostile attacks and depredations of the Indians. The extent to which this should be attempted is of course left to your own discretion, keeping in view the leading object of the Campaign.

In reference to the civil affairs of the Territory of Arizona it is not the desire of the General that the Government instituted and established by Lt. Col. Baylor should be in any manner disturbed and your powers are limited to the military operations.

To   I am Colonel
Col. J. Reily   your obt Servt.
Com^{dg} 4th Regt. T.M.V.
     San Antonio Tex.   Ass. Adjt. Genl.

50.

Hd. Qrs. Sibley Brigade A.G.O.
San Antonio Tex. Oct. 23rd 61

General:

I request your attention to a matter of some importance to the equipment of this Command and perhaps to the successful accomplishment of the duty with which I am charged.

Upon being directed by the President to raise and organize this force, I was empowered by him to call upon the officer in command of this Department for all the necessary supplies and equipment, and in particular for a Battery of Eight 12-pounder Howitzers known to be among the Ordnance here. This authority, although verbal, was promptly recognized by Genl. Van Dorn, until recently in command of the Department, who verbally directed the Battery (Eight pieces) to be delivered to me when called for. Four of the Guns have been heretofore called for and received, but I am just advised by the endorsement of Col. H. E. McCulloch acting in command here, upon a requisition put in by my Ordnance Officer, that the remainder will not be turned over to this Command, although they are a portion of those so directed by Genl. Van Dorn.

Up to this time I have acquiesced in the somewhat anomalous position of Col. McCulloch, exercising the powers of Commander of the Department, and I should not cease to do so now but that I consider his action in this matter as very prejudicial to the public interest and possibly placing in jeopardy the success of my expedition. Two more of those Guns are indispensable to arm my Battery, which was originally designed to consist of Eight pieces [incomplete; one or more pages missing].
[marginal note: "not send"]

51.

Hd. Qrs. Sibley Brig: A.G.O.
San Antonio Tex. Oct. 31st 1861

Captain:

General Sibley directs that you will at once proceed to the City of Austin for the purpose of procuring Pistols (six shooters) to supply the deficiency existing in your Company.

The General empowers you to make purchases of Pistols upon the best terms you can effect, to be paid for by the Quartermaster of the Brigade so soon as he returns, which he is expected to do in a week or ten days.

I am Captain
your obt Servt.

Capt. J. B. McCown
San Antonio Tex.   Ass. Adjt. Genl.

52.

Hd. Qrs. Sibley Brig: A.G.O.
San Antonio Tex: Nov. 1st 1861

Colonel.

Your communication of the 30th ult. to Genl. Sibley, in regard to the organization of the Field Artillery attached to your Regiment, has been considered by him, and I am instructed in reply to inform you that while he concurs in the expediency of your recommendations, yet some legal difficulties may arise from exercising the appointing power which they suggest.

The Men to serve the Battery being obtained by detail from troops already in the service, they cannot be organized into a separate Company, and they [*sic*] Enabled to elect their own officers. On the other hand it is understood that the power of the President to appoint officers to command Volunteer forces is limited to Field Officers and does not apply to those of Companies.

In view notwithstanding, however, the difficulties thus presenting themselves, the General, in view of the great importance which he attaches to the efficient organization of this Detachment, is willing to go as far as he feels authorized towards giving effect to your recommendations, and has accordingly conferred upon Mr. W. S. Wood the appointment of Acting 1st Lieutenant (subject to the approval of his Excellency the President) and has ordered him to duty with the Field Artillery of your Regiment. If Mr. Wood accepts, he must do so with a full premonition of the doubts in regard to the validity of the appointment and of the approval of the President, taking all the risk upon himself, both in regard to pay and otherwise.

If Mr. Fulchrod [Fulcrod] is willing to accept the appointment of Acting 2nd Lieutenant upon the same terms, the General will appoint him to that position in like manner.

On the 22nd of September last, you were informed of the details necessary for the service of the Battery—viz: two Sergts., two Corporals and thirty Privates.

To Col. Thos. Green   [no signature block]
    Comdg 5th Regt. T.M.V.

53.

Hd. Qrs. Sibley Brigade A.G.O.
San Antonio Tex: Nov. 5th 1861

Brig. Genl. P. O. Hébert
    General:

You are no doubt apprised that I am organizing at this place a Brigade of Cavalry for service in New Mexico, for the supplies for which, "Quartermaster's, Commissary, and Ordnance Stores," I was empowered by the President to call on the Comdg Officer of this Military Department. Accordingly while there was a Commanding Officer at this place I encountered no serious obstacles in obtaining for my command such supplies as could be furnished from the Depots here. My requisitions were made on such officers and were filled as far as he deemed it practicable.

I am now informed, however, that Colonel McCulloch has been relieved by yourself from the position he has recently occupied at this place of Acting Commander of the Department, and that there is no officer here authorized to direct issues from any of the Depots here. I am further informed that you may still be detained a considerable time by your duties at Galveston.

Under those circumstances, the exigencies of the service render it important imperative [*sic*] on me to assume the responsibility of ordering such issues from the Depots here as are indispensable for my command, and as can be spared from there without prejudice to the requirements of the Department for its own service. One of my Regiments is already on the march; another is under marching orders; and the third will be put under such orders in a few days. It is thus impracticable for me to await, as I would prefer to do, such arrangements to be made by your orders as would obviate the necessity on my part of assuming such responsibility.

It has been my careful policy heretofore, and still is my desire to avoid most scrupulously the slightest interference with the powers of the Commander of the Dept. I am confident that the circumstances which I now communicate to you will justify my present action in your opinion.

To Brig. Genl. P. O. Hébert   [no signature block]
    Com^{dg} Dept. of Texas
    Galveston Texas.

54.

Hd. Qrs. Sibley Brigade A.G.O.
San Antonio Tex. Nov. 7th 61

General S. Cooper
Adjt. & Insp. Genl. C.S.A.
    General.

On the 30th of Sept. last, I informed you that I had appointed Lieut. Arthur Shaaff Ordnance Officer of my command conferring upon him subject to the approval of his Excellency the President, the rank of Captain. From his military education and experience I expected his appointment would prove an efficient and satisfactory one. For reasons, however, not necessary to detail, it proved otherwise, in view of which and of Lieut. Shaaff's own request I relieved him on the 21st day of October, and assigned to the Ordnance Service of the Brigade my Volunteer Aid de Camp, Willis L. Robards, Esq., of Austin in this State.

This gentleman early in the organization of this command tendered me his services as Volunteer Aid, and I have found him in the several responsible and difficult capacities in which I have employed him a most ready, indefatigable, and efficient officer, sparing no pains, although looking to no recompense, to discharge the duties thus imposed upon him in the most satisfactory manner.

He has not only filled the position of Ordnance Officer since Lt. Shaaff was relieved up to this time, but he is now and for nearly two weeks has been discharging the duties of both the Quartermaster and Commissary of the Brigade, in the absence of Capt. Harrison A.Q.M. and Major Brownrigg A.C.S. whom I found it necessary to dispatch to New Orleans. The complicated, difficult, and important duties of those several departments he conducts in a manner most efficient and satisfactory. His personal character is held in the highest esteem by a numerous circle of acquaintances.

The personal obligations which I feel that he has imposed upon me by the very valuable assistance he has rendered and is still rendering, and the capacity which he displays of making a most efficient staff officer, impel me to recommend him, as I now strongly do, for an appointment as Ordnance Officer to this Brigade with the highest rank admissible in such an appointment. I shall stand in great need, throughout his service assigned to me, of an efficient officer in this capacity, and I am confident that the gentleman would be a valuable acquisition to this or any other command in the Ordnance or any other Department to which he might be attached.

It is due to him to state that I prefer this request for his appointment from no importunity, request, or even suggestion of his, but simply for the reasons I have stated.

I beg leave further to request that inasmuch as the grade of Major has been conferred upon the Adjutant General and Commissary of the Brigade, that the same rank be given to the Brigade Quartermaster, Captain Harrison, to date from the original appointment.

To Brig. Genl. S. Cooper   [no signature block]
    Adjt. & Insp. Genl. C.S.A.
       Richmond Va.

55.

Hd. Qrs. Sibley Brig: A.G.O.
San Antonio Tex: Nov. 8th 61

Genl. S. Cooper
Adjt. & Insp. Genl. C.S.A.

General.

I have the honor to forward herewith for your information certain letters from Lt. Col. Baylor, Judge Crosby and Judge Hart relative to military movements on both sides in the Territory of New Mexico.

I regard the probable advance of the Federal forces there as a movement decidedly to be desired by us, and that so soon as my force shall reach the field of action, it must result in the destruction or capture of the enemy's force. It is no doubt induced by the threatened attack of Lt. Col. Baylor on Fort Craig, made by my order.

Col. Reily's Regiment of my Brigade is by this time some two hundred and fifty miles *en route*. Col. Green's broke camp yesterday, and my Third Regiment (Col. Steele's) will follow very soon. Not an hour shall be lost in pushing forward the whole force. The delays heretofore encountered have been unavoidable.

Messrs. Crosby and Hart are engaged under my authority in procuring supplies for my command, which I state here as explanatory of their letters.

To Genl. S. Cooper   [no signature block]
Adjt. & Insp. Genl. C.S.A.[1]

56.

Hd. Qrs. Sibley Brig: A.G.O.
San Antonio Tex: Nov. 10th 1861

General S. Cooper
Adjutant & Insp. Genl. C.S.A.

General.

I have the honor to report the following appointments made by me subject to the approval of his Excellency the President. If they are confirmed, I beg leave to suggest that the Commissions *should bear date* from the *dates* at which they *were* made by me, inasmuch as those officers entered at those [dates] upon the discharge of their respective duties. The appointments heretofore made and confirmed have been thus made to bear date from your office, and I beg that you will, in justice to those officers, cause their appointments to be dated in the same manner.

This list comprises all the appointments up to this date except those heretofore communicated.

Arthur P. Bagby, Major of Col. Wm Steele's Regiment (Sibley Brigade) T.M.V. appointed October 12th 61.

M. L. Ogden Assistant Quartermaster to Col. Wm Steele's Regiment (Sibley Brigade) T.M.V. appointed November 5th 1861.

M. A. Southworth M.D., Surgeon appointed September 13th 1861.

L. M. Taylor M.D., Assistant Surgeon appointed August 29th 1861, and

J. F. Machet M.D., Assistant Surgeon appointed October 7th 1861 to Colonel James Reily's 4th Regiment T.M.V.

F. Bracht M.D., Surgeon appointed September 13th 1861.

J. M. Bronaugh, Assistant Surgeon appointed October 7th 1861, and

J. R. McPhaill M.D., Assistant Surgeon appointed October 7th 1861 to Colonel Thomas Green's 5th Regiment T.M.V.

G. Cupples M.D., Surgeon appointed October 22nd 1861.

J. W. Cunningham M.D., Assistant Surgeon appointed October 22nd 1861, and

T. B. Greenwood M.D., Assistant Surgeon appointed October 22nd 1861 to Colonel William Steele's Regiment (Sibley Brigade) T.M.V.

	I have the honor to be
To	General,
Genl. S. Cooper	Very respectfully
Adjt. & Insp. Genl. C.S.A.	your obt Servt.
Richmond Va.	(Signed) H. H. Sibley
	Brig. Genl. P.C.S.A.

Note

In addition to the above I have the honor to request that the appointment of Marion B. Hyatt as Assistant Quartermaster with the rank of Captain to Colonel Thomas Green's Regiment 5th T.M.V. be approved to date from November 8th 61.

(Signed)   H. H. Sibley
Brig. Genl. Com^{dg}

57.

Hd. Qrs. Sibley Brigade A.G.O.
San Antonio Tex: Nov. 10th 61

General S. Cooper
Adjt. & Insp. Genl. C.S.A.

General.

I have the honor herewith to transmit one copy each of the original Muster Rolls of the twenty Companies composing the 4th and 5th Regts. of Texas Mounted Volunteers, being the 1st and 2nd of this Brigade.

The delay in forwarding these rolls has arisen from the failure of the Mustering Officers to return promptly the Rolls to this office.

The Muster Rolls of Colonel Steele's (the Third) Regiment of this Brigade will be transmitted as soon as the organization of the Regiment is complete, to which one Company is still necessary and daily expected.

The Mustering Officers were appointed by Special Orders 9, 17 and 38 of Brig. Genl. Sibley, which will appear among the orders of which transcripts are forwarded under separate cover.

I have the honor to be
General,

To   Very respectfully
Genl. S. Cooper   your obt Servt.
Adjt. & Insp. Genl. C.S.A.   (Signed)   A. M. Jackson
Richmond Va.   Asst. Adjt. Genl.

58.

Hd. Qrs. Sibley Brigade A.G.O.
San Antonio Tex: Nov. 11th 1861

Lt. Colonel R. B. [*sic*] Baylor
Com^{dg} in Arizonia
    Colonel.

I am directed by Brig. Genl. Sibley to acknowledge the receipt of your communication to him of date of Oct. 25th 1861.

The General instructs me to reply that he is pushing forward his troops with all possible dispatch. The 1st Regiment of this Brigade (Col. James Reily's) has been some time en route, and it will probably arrive at El Paso by the 1st of the ensuing month at the latest. Col. Reily is making all possible expedition.

The 2nd Regiment of the Brigade (Col. Thos. Green) is also on the march, and camps to night at Castroville. The 3rd Regiment (Col. Wm Steele's) will take up the line of march in a very few days. The General himself with his Hd. Quarters will move very soon, at the earliest possible day, and make all practicable speed to El Paso.

The General has every confidence that you will do every thing of which your small force is capable to hold the enemy in check until his arrival.

I am, Colonel
your obt Servt.
To
Colonel R. B. Baylor   (Signed) A. M. Jackson
    Com^{dg} in Arizonia   Ass. Adjt. Genl.

59.

Hd. Qrs. Sibley Brigade A.G.O.
San Antonio Tex: Nov. 13th 61

Lt. Col. J. Gorgas
Chief of Ordnance C.S.A.

Sir:

Under date of Oct. 3rd 1861, you addressed me a communication in reference to certain accounts in favor of Mr. G. H. Giddings for Arms furnished by him for my command. I am not informed in that communication that any disposition has been made of those accounts, and presume its object was to elicit such explanation as I might be able to give in regard to them.

In reply therefore, I have to state that in raising this Command by order of his Excellency, the President, I found that in every company which offered itself for the Service great deficiencies of Arms existed. Every company reported that they had brought all the serviceable Arms they could procure in the sections where they were raised, and I have every reason to believe those representations were true.

To provide for these deficiencies I in the first place made the proper inquiries of the Military Dept., and then of the State Government, whether they would be able to furnish the Arms necessary and in reply I learned that they were not. No alternative remained but to procure them by purchase. Mr. Giddings under these circumstances offered me his services to procure them, and I accepted them without hesitation. He was already the Agent of the Government for a similar purpose, and in every other respect a very fit and competent person. The accounts to which you refer are for the Arms furnished by him for the purpose already stated.

It does not appear to me to be very material whether his action in this matter is to be considered as within the purview of the authority already conferred upon him by the Government, or as attributable to my authority alone. The accomplishment of the objects charged upon me by the President and the unserviceable condition of my Troops, made it indispensable to purchase those Arms, the only way they were procurable. To have rejected the Companies because they were deficient in Arms would have been equivalent to an abandonment of the duty assigned me of raising this Brigade, for there was no hope that other Companies better supplied could be obtained.

In view of these undoubted facts I cannot believe that the propriety of my action will be questioned, nor that provision will be refused, for the payments of the liabilities incurred.

It may be supposed that I should have applied to the Department at Richmond before pursuing the course I did. With every disposition to have done so, if practicable, such an application would have involved a delay which would have completely paralyzed my command for the winter, have disabled me perhaps from accomplishing the objects of my expedition, and have inevitably resulted in a much heavier expenditure by the Government than will now be incurred.

I further state that besides the purchases from Mr. Giddings I have been compelled for the same reasons to make many others, and some at what may appear exorbitant prices. And notwithstanding all the purchases made, I have been necessitated to have Lances made to complete the equipment of my Troops. For all the liabilities thus incurred I hope provision will be made.

While on this subject I further state that I have appointed an Agent at El Paso (Hon. J. F. Crosby) to obtain by contract or purchase Ammunition for the future supply of my Command. A sufficient amount for the estimated wants of my Brigade could not be obtained here.

	I am Colonel
To	Very respectfully
Lt. Col. J. Gorgas	your obt Servt.
Chief of Ord. C.S.A.	(Signed) H. H. Sibley
Richmond Va.	Brig. Genl. C.S.A.

60.

Hd. Qrs. Sibley Brig. A.G.O.
San Antonio Tex: Nov. 16th 61

Captain W. H. Harrison
    A.Q.M. Sibley Brig.
Captain.

The Genl. Com[dg] orders you on your arrival at this place with funds of your Department, to pay off and discharge out of them all the outstanding debts as well of the Ordnance Officers of this Brigade, or other approved liabilities, as of your own Department. The funds so expended and applied to other liabilities than those pertaining to your Department, will be returned by transfer as soon as the Ordnance Service is placed in funds, which have been estimated for.

By order of Genl Sibley
(Signed)   A. M. Jackson
Ass. Adjt. Genl.

61.

Hd. Qrs. Sibley Brigade A.G.O.
San Antonio Texas Nov. 17th 61

Genl. S. Cooper
Adjt. & Insp. Genl. C.S.A.
    General.

I have the honor to report that on Monday next, the 18th inst., I shall move with my Head Quarters to assume in person the command of our forces in the Territory of Arizona, and to conduct the military operations there and in New Mexico.

Before proceeding to this distant field of duty, it appears proper that I should briefly communicate to you such facts concerning my official transactions here, and touching the present condition of my forces, as may be necessary for the information of your office.

On my arrival here about the middle of August last, I confidently expected to be able to raise and organize my Brigade within a very brief space of time, and to have been enabled by this date to have it actively employed in the accomplishment of the objects for which it was raised. Many unexpected circumstances, however, have concurred to defeat this expectation.

In the first place I was disappointed in not receiving from the Executive of this State as efficient co-operation as was desirable. This arose from no want of disposition or zeal on the part of Gov. Clark to render every facility in his power for the rapid organization of the force called for. It was the consequence simply of the very inefficient system of the State military organization to which the Governor had recourse to supply the Troops. He ordered a sufficient number of Companies which had reported to him as organized, to report to me for the Service of this Brigade; but the most of these Companies had, as it appeared, either entirely disbanded, or their numbers had become diminished below the minimum of the Confederate Service. The reliance, therefore, which was placed in this mode of raising the men caused the first serious delay.

In the second place, the designation by the Governor of Companies organized under the State law, operated to deter other Companies not so organized from offering their services to me, which many would have done at once but for the opinion very generally prevalent that the Brigade would be filled by the Companies ordered out by the Governor. Although at the very earliest day that it became apparent that the Companies ordered out by the Governor could not be relied on, I at once resorted direct to the people themselves, yet it required some time to counteract the effects of the misplaced reliance upon the State system.

Another cause of delay arose from the competition for men which grew out of the calls for the several Regiments required for the Service east of the Mississippi.

I enumerate these sources of delay simply to explain the unexpected detentions which I have encountered, and not as implying any imputations upon any one whatever.

Although I am advancing to the field of duty assigned to me with the confident hope of being able to accomplish every thing designed there by his Excellency the President, yet it is proper that I should state that very great deficiencies still exist in the arms of the troops, notwithstanding every effort on my part to obviate them. Every Company reported itself short of arms, and gave the sufficient reason that they were not to be procured in their respective sections, partly in consequence of the drain already made upon the people, and partly in consequence of the great reluctance of the people to allow the serviceable arms to be removed from the State, for the defense of whose coast it was generally believed they would shortly be required. The difficulty thus arising had to be surmounted in some manner. Neither this Military Department nor the State Government supplied the deficiency.

Wherefore in virtue of the authority delegated to me in the written instructions of his Excellency the President, I directed the purchase of serviceable fire-arms and the construction of lances. There not being a dollar in the hands of any of the disbursing officers of my command, I was necessitated to resort to the credit of the Government for these purchases. The liabilities are outstanding, and on the 13th of the present month I enclosed to the Chief of Ordnance the estimates of the funds necessary for their liquidation.

To another matter I desire to invite your attention. Shortly after my arrival here, Genl. Van Dorn was relieved from duty as Commander of this Department, and Col. H. McCulloch was left in that position. Brig. Genl. Hébert came within the limits of this Department, but did not come on to its Hd. Qrs. and assume the command, but up to very recently left Col. McCulloch to act in that capacity, as far at least as the depots and military affairs of this place and section were concerned. Maj. Macklin, A.Q.M. and acting Ordnance Officer of this Dept., left this place to meet Genl. Hébert at Galveston, and still remains there. Col. McCulloch shortly afterwards also left for the same purpose, and the intelligence was soon returned that he had been relieved of the command of the Department by the General. The General has not yet come on here.

The consequence of all this is, that there is and for the last two or three weeks has been no off. within my reach to who I could apply for the issues of Ordnance Stores absolutely necessary for my command. In this situation I assumed the responsibility of ordering and requiring from the subordinates in charge of the Ordnance Stores here, the issuance of such Ordnance Stores as were indispensable to my command as could be spared from the Service of the Department itself. On assuming this responsibility I immediately communicated the fact to Genl. Hébert at Galveston, with the reasons and motives for my action, but have as yet received no reply from him. Not to have taken this responsibility would have been to incur another and an indefinite delay, which would have probably paralyzed my command for the winter, and would certainly have disabled me from arriving at El Paso, as I hope to do in time to succor the small force there under Col. Baylor, whose communications regarding an immediate attack by a greatly superior force I forwarded to you on the 8th inst.

These facts will, I trust vindicate me from any imputation of unwarrantable intrusion upon the powers of the Dept. Commander, which I have been scrupulous to avoid.

The 4th Regt. (Col. Reily's) being the 1st of this Brigade, took up the line of march on the 22nd of last month, and at last advices was making rapid progress. The 5th Regt. (Col. Green's) being my 2nd , took up the march on the 2nd inst, and will make all possible dispatch. I hope to arrive at El Paso in time to overtake my advanced Corps. Col. Steele's Regt. is just now completely organized, and will probably be able to march by the 20th inst.

[no signature block][2]

62.

Hd. Qrs. Sibley Brigade A.G.O.
San Antonio Texas. Nov. 18th 61

Col. W. L. Robards
Act. Ord. Officer S.B.
    Sir:
    The General Commanding directs that you will remain at this place in the discharge of the duties of the Officers of A.Q.M. and A.C.S. of the Brigade, with which you have been temporarily charged until relieved therefrom by the regular officers of these Departments. Whereupon you will rejoin the Hd Qrs. either by stage, or in company with the Third Regt. or any detachments of this command going is [sic] destination of Hd. Qrs. In the latter course the A.Q.M. of this Brigade will provide you with the proper transportation.
    If you deem it advisable to take the stage, the expenses attending it will be paid by the A.Q.M. of the Brigade.

Very respectfully
(Signed)   A. M. Jackson
Ass. Adjt. Genl.

63.

Hd. Qrs. Army of New Mexico A.G.O.
Fort Bliss Tex: Dec. 16th 1861

General S. Cooper
Adjt. & Insp. Genl. C.S.A.

General.

I have the honor to report that I arrived at this Post on the 14th inst. and have for the present established here my Head Quarters.

Col. Reily's Regiment, 4th Tex. Mt. Vols., has just reached this vicinity and will be temporarily encamped a few miles above this point.

Col. Green's Regt., 5th Tex. Mt. Vols., is expected next week.

I am informed by letter from Col. Steele, 7th T.M.V., that five Companies of his Regiment took up the line of march from San Antonio, on the 28th ult. No doubt the balance of his Regiment are *en route* several days since.

I address you other communications, one informing you of certain appointments made by me: The others concerning certain proclamations which I have promulgated, and communications addressed by me to the Governors of the States of Chihuahua and Sonora.

I have the honor, General
to be your obt Servt.

Brig. Genl. C.S.A.
Comdg Army of N.M.

P.S. Reliable advices have been received by me by expresses dispatched by my direction, that no Federal troops have been landed at Guaymas or elsewhere in the Mexican States.

64.

Hd. Qrs. Army of New Mexico
Fort Bliss Tex: Dec. 16th 1861

Genl. S. Cooper
Adjt. & Insp. Genl. C.S.A.

General.

I have the honor to communicate that, subject to the approval of his Excellency the President, I have this day appointed Lieut. Colonel John R. Baylor to be a Colonel in the Provisional Army; Captain Peter Hardeman to be Lieutenant Colonel to supply the vacancy occasioned by the promotion of Col. Baylor; and Major Edwin Waller Jr. to be Lieutenant Colonel. All these Officers previous to their promotions belonged to the 2nd Regt. (Col. Ford's) Texas Mt. Rifles.

The gallant and important services rendered by them in their operations in Arizona during the past few months, constituted, it appeared to me, a claim for the exercise of the powers conferred upon me by his Excellency the President, which could not be disregarded. Into the details of these services I feel it unnecessary to enter, inasmuch as they are already matters of history.

But besides this consideration of their high merits, a very cogent military reason existed in the fact that, unless these appointments were made, a very serious and embarrassing question might at any day have arisen between Col. Ford and myself, inasmuch as they and their commands still constituted a portion of his Regiment.

I am thus particular in giving the reasons for my action, for the reason that I should regret nothing more than that, for want of information, I should be supposed in the slightest degree to have abused the high powers entrusted to me by his Excellency the President.

I beg therefore that the Commissions bearing date from this day be forwarded to these gentlemen. Those of Col. Baylor and Lieut. Colonel Hardeman to these Head Quarters. That of Lieut. Colonel Waller to Hempstead, Texas, to which place he has been ordered to raise and organize a battalion of six companies.

I have the honor, General
to be your obt Servt.
(Signed)   H. H. Sibley
Brig. Genl. C.S.A.
Com^{dg} Army of N.M.

65.

El Paso Texas
Dec. 17th 1861

A. F. Wulff Esq.
Sir:

Your proposition to furnish the Army under my command with 5000 lbs. of powder is accepted.

Captain Holliday will proceed to Presidio del Norte in the course of two days, for the purpose of receiving and taking charge of the same. Captain Holliday will be fully authorized to receive and receipt for the quantity delivered to him, and on the presentation of your account at Head Quarters at this place, payment for the same will be made.

Respectfully
your obt Servt.
(Signed)   H. H. Sibley
Brig. Genl. Com^{dg}

66.

Hd. Qrs. Army of New Mexico
Fort Bliss Tex: Dec. 17th 61

Genl. S. Cooper
Adjt. & Insp. Genl. C.S.A.

General:

I have the honor to report that I have this day, in the exercise of the powers conferred upon me by his Excellency the President, and subject to his approval, appointed Henry E. Loebnitz to be Quarter Master of the 4th Regiment (Col. Reily's) Texas Mounted Vols., with the rank of Captain.

This officer was previously a Second Lieutenant of Captain Hampton's Company "C" of the same Regiment, but has been since shortly after the organization of the Regiment acting [as] its Quarter Master. The remarkable capacity and fidelity with which he has discharged his duties made his regular appointment to it a matter of simple justice.

If approved by his Excellency, I request that Captain Loebnitz's Commission, to bear date from this date, be transmitted to these Head Quarters.

I have the honor, General,
to be your obt. Servt.
(Signed)   H. H. Sibley
Brig. Genl. C.S.A.
Comdg Army of N.M.

67.

Hd. Qrs. Army of New Mexico A.G.O.
Fort Bliss Texas Dec. 19th 1861

Colonel.

The General Commanding directs that you will detach two Companies, the freshest of your Regiment, under command of Lt. Colonel Scurry, to report to Colonel J. R. Baylor at Messilla [*sic*] for reconnoitering duty.

I am Colonel
Very respectfully

To   (Signed)   A. M. Jackson
Col. James Reily   Asst. Adjt. Genl.
Com^{dg} 4th Regt. T.M.V.   Army of New Mexico

68.

Hd. Qrs. Army of New Mexico
Fort Bliss Tex. Dec. 20th 61

Col. Jno. R. Baylor
Messilla Ar.

Colonel.

By direction of the Genl. Com^{dg} I enclose you a copy of a communication received by him from Mr. J. B. Lacoste in reference to the condition and operations of his firm of Sweet and Lacoste at the Copper Mines in Arizona.

In consideration of the fact that it may become a matter of much importance to the Government to obtain supplies of this mineral from this source, you are directed to inquire into the matters referred to by Mr. Lacoste, and to afford him all the just protection in your power against molestation or injury in this business.

I am Colonel
Your obt Servt.
(Signed)   A. M. Jackson
Ass. Adjt. Genl.
Army of N.M.

69.

Hd. Qrs, Army of New Mexico AGO
Fort Bliss Tex. Dec. 21, 61

To His Excellency the
    Governor of the State of Chihuahua.
Sir

Upon assuming command of the military forces of the Confederate States upon this frontier, I deem it of the first importance to come, if possible, to a frank and cordial agreement with the government of the contiguous Mexican States in regard to certain matters which will necessarily concern the future relations of our respective Republics.

In opening communication with your Excellency upon these subjects, it is my first and most agreeable duty, to assure you, as I most sincerely do that the Government of the Confederate States and of the State of Texas are solicitous of cultivating with the Mexican Republic and the several states composing it, relations not merely of peace, but of amity and good will. The maintenance of such relations is a manifest necessity to the political and commercial well being of countries whose common boundaries and mutual intercourse are so extensive as those of the Northern States of Mexico and the Confederate States. Nothing shall be omitted on my part to inaugurate and preserve, so far as in my opinion this policy of my government and I entertain the hope that reciprocal motives will actuate yourself, Sir, and other high functionaries entrusted with the public affairs of the States of Mexico.

Entertaining these views, I regret to be compelled to ask your Excellency's attention to certain statements which purport to emanate from the public journals of the cities of Mexico and Vera Cruz to the effect that by some treaty or convention entered into within the last few months by the Central Government of Mexico and the Federal Government of the United States, the right has been conceded by the former to the latter to march troops and munitions of war across the territories of the Mexican States for the purpose of employing such troops and munitions of war in the war now pending between the United States and the Confederate States. It is incumbent upon me to ask from your Excellency an explanation whether or not such a treaty or convention exists or is recognized and respected by the Government of his State of Chihuahua. If your Excellency shall apprise me that such a right has been conceded to the Enemy with whom my Government is at war, and that such a right is respected by the Government of your State, the further duty will devolve upon me of informing your Excellency, in a future communication, of the consequences which are to be apprehended in case the United States shall attempt to avail themselves of his facilities so afforded them to the injury of the States I have the honor to serve.

I consider it proper to communicate officially to your Excellency, as I have now the honor of doing, the fact that the forces under my command have now, and for some time have had full possession of the region of country known as Arizona and comprising the towns and settlements of the Mesilla Valley. It is no doubt a fact well known to your Excellency that the Settlements of Arizona have long been subject to frequent incursions from the hostile Indians who infest this frontier to the great injury of your people as well as ours. These Indians upon committing depredations within one jurisdiction have been in the habit of seeking refuge with the other. It appears to me that a system of co-operation can be easily devised between your Excellency and myself by which without the least offence or injury to our respective governments or people an ample retribution can be inflicted upon these enemies of the human race. I propose to you that the troops of either Government shall be at liberty to pursue them within the territory of the other, the pursuing force to report as early as practicable their purpose and strength to the nearest military post of the country within which it shall have intruded. By concerted action of our respective forces upon such a base, it would seem certain that these predatory tribes can be effectually subjugated or exterminated. Should this proposition meet your Excellency's concurrence, I shall hold myself ready to embody it in any more solemn form that may be preferred by you.

During the operation of my Army, it may become expedient for me to endeavor to procure by purchase from the markets of Chihuahua supplies for my force. In that case, I entertain the hope that the convention recognized and practiced between friendly governments will be extended to my agents.

#Added to letter to Governor of Sonora

#I would be pleased if your Excellency would concede to me the right under such reasonable regulations as you may desire of establishing a depot in the port of Guaymas and of a transient from thence through the territory of your State. It is easy to see the immense advantages which must in a very brief period accrue to your people from such facilities and I am prepared to give you, in any form you may suggest, the amplest guarantee that they shall not be abused.

With great respect and the highest consid.
I am your Excellency's most obt Servt.

(Signed)   H. H. Sibley

Brig. Gen. Comdg.

70.

Hd. Qrs. Army of New Mexico A.G.O.
Fort Bliss Texas. Dec. 21st 1861

Genl. S. Cooper
Adjt. & Insp. Genl. C.S.A.
     General.
     I have the honor to enclose for your information copies of two proclamations promulgated by me, and also copies of communications officially addressed by me to the Governors of the contiguous Mexican States of Chihuahua and Sonora.

                         I have the honor, General
                         To be your obt. Servt.
          (Signed)   H. H. Sibley
                         Brig. Genl. C.S.A.
                         Com^{dg} Army of N.M.

P.S. I enclose also for your information a copy of my General Order assuming the command of all the troops in this section. You will perceive it includes Fort Quitman and this post. Owing to the immediate connection between this section and Arizona, and the necessity of maintaining a military control over the Settlements between Messilla and Fort Quitman, for the purpose of screening my movements from the enemy, this was absolutely necessary, for the present at least, and I hope therefore it will be approved.

71.

Hd. Qrs. Army of New Mexico A.G.O.
Fort Bliss Tex: Dec. 23rd 1861

Colonel J. Reily
Com^{dg} 4th Regt. T.M.V.

Colonel.

The General Comdg is desirous of opening communication, through the medium of an officer of high rank, with the Governors of the States of Chihuahua and Sonora, on subjects of great importance both to the operations of this Army and to the future relations of these States with the Confederate States.

In consideration of your rank and of your experience as a diplomatist, the General has selected you for this important duty.

You are therefore directed to report in person to the General Commanding, with as little delay as possible, for the purpose of conference in regard to this subject.

You will of course turn over the command of your Regiment, temporarily, to the next officer in rank or seniority.

I am, Colonel
Your obt Servt.
(Signed)   A. M. Jackson
Ass. Adjt. Genl.

72.

Hd. Qrs. Army of New Mexico
Fort Bliss Tex: Dec. 24th 1861

Colonel J. R. Baylor
Com^{dg} at Messilla

Colonel.

The General Com^{dg} directs me to inform you that he has countermanded an order given by you for the transportation from this Post to Messilla of a quantity of clothing now here.

The General found this necessary in view of the destitution of some of the troops now en route for this place.

I am, Colonel
Your obt. Servt.
(Signed)   A. M. Jackson
Ass. Adjt. Genl.

[unrelated marginal note dated Dec. 11, 1881, not included]

73.

Hd. Qrs. Army of New Mexico A.G.O.
Fort Bliss Texas. Dec. 24th 1861

Col. J. R. Baylor
Com^{dg} C.S. Forces
Messilla

Colonel:

Your despatch covering the communication of Lt. Col. B. S. Roberts, U.S.A., commanding at Fort Craig, proposing an exchange of prisoners, has been received.

The General Commanding, actuated by the same motives of humanity so laudably influencing Col. Roberts, directs that the proposed exchange be made. You will take the proper steps for effecting the exchange, and furnish such papers releasing the parole of the prisoner in New Mexico, as may be satisfactory to Capt. Selden.

I am, Colonel,
Your obt. Servt.
(Signed)   A. M. Jackson
Ass. Adjt. Genl.
Army of New Mexico

74.

Hd. Qrs. Army of New Mexico A.G.O.
Fort Bliss Tex: Dec. 25th 1861

Col. J. R. Baylor
Com^{dg} C.S. Forces
Messilla
    Colonel:
    The Genl. Com^{dg} directs that you will make the reconoisance [*sic*] heretofore ordered at the first moment consistent with good faith towards the enemy and the flag of truce.

I am, Colonel,
Your obt. Servt.
(Signed)   A. M. Jackson
Ass. Adjt. Genl.
Army of New Mexico

[unrelated note dated Dec. 11, 1881, not included]

75.

Hd. Qrs. Army of New Mexico A.G.O.
Fort Bliss Tex: Dec. 27th 1861

To His Excellency
    Governor of the State of Chihuahua
        Sir:

I have the honor hereby to accredit to your Excellency Colonel James Reily of the Army of the Confederate States, who is charged with the duty of delivering to your Excellency a communication of importance and of further explaining the views entertained by and objects contemplated by me.

Col. Reily is the next officer to myself in rank and command, present on this frontier with the forces of the Confederate States, and your Excellency will recognize in his selection for this duty, the desire I have of manifesting to you my high respect and appreciation.

I commend to your consideration the representations which he shall make you, and bespeak for him your highest confidence and esteem as well in his private as in his official capacity.

                    With great respect and the
                    highest consideration, I am
                    your Excellency's most obt Servt.
        (Signed)   H. H. Sibley
                    Brig. Genl. C.S.A.
                    Commanding[3]

76.

Hd. Qrs. Army of New Mexico
Fort Bliss Tex: Dec. 30th 1861

Mr. Monigle
Agent of San Antonio Mail Co. El Paso Texas
    Sir:
    I am directed by Genl. H. H. Sibley Com^{dg} to say to you that
if you will transport by stage to San Antonio, Mr. B. B. Sax[t]on
and G. C. Blackburn, he will direct their fare to be paid by the Qr.
Master of this Army on his arrival.

> I am your obt Servt.
> (Signed)   A. M. Jackson
> Ass. Adjt. Genl. Army of N.M.

77.

Hd. Qrs. Army of New Mexico
Fort Bliss Tex: Dec. 31st 1861

Col. James Reily
4th Regt. T.M.V.
Colonel:
    The General Com^{dg} directs me to communicate to you the
objects he has in view and which he purposes to effect through the
mission for which you have been selected.
    Your first duty will be to proceed to the City of Chihuahua,
and to deliver in person to the Gov. of that State the
communication addressed to him by the General, of the contents
of which you have already been apprized. In that communication
it has of course only been practicable to explain to the Gov. the
general outline of the policy and the general nature of the objects
which are at present in contemplation. To unfold that policy and
to explain these objects in detail, to further their accomplishment,
to counteract any adverse influence and to obviate any possible
objections—these are the chief and primary duties devolved upon

you. The mode and manner of discharging this duty is of course left to your own judgment and discretion.

You will also call to the attention of the Governor the exaction of duties by the Custom House Officer at El Paso from Citizens of this place, removing their goods &c. there for temporary security a few weeks since; and ask that such duties be remitted to the parties who paid them.

You will be accompanied by the Vol. Aid de Camp of the General, Captain J. Dwyer, of whose zeal, intelligence and accomplishments you can avail yourself in your intercourse with the officials with who you will be brought in contact. This assistance you will find valuable in many respects, and his association the General hopes will prove an agreeable one to each.

Should a safe opportunity offer, you will report, as early as possible, the nature of the reception given you and the prospects of a favorable adjustment of the matters entrusted to your charge.

Should you after discharging your mission at Chihuahua, arrive at the conclusion from such information as you can there obtain that it is expedient and promotive of the public interest for you to proceed to Sonora, you will do so. Otherwise you will arrange for the transmission to the Governor of that State of the official communication of the General.

Upon the completion of your mission, you will report in person to the Genl. Com^{dg}.

> I am, Colonel,
> your obt. Servt.
>
> (Signed)   A. M. Jackson
> Ass. Adjt. Genl.
> Army of New Mexico[4]

78.

Hd. Qrs. Army of New Mexico
Fort Bliss Tex: Dec. 31st 61

General S. Cooper
Adjt. & Insp. Genl. C.S.A.

General:

I have the honor of enclosing to you the resignations of several Company officers belonging to the Brigade of Cavalry organized by Brig. Genl. H. H. Sibley at San Antonio Tex. viz:

1. W. H. Harris	1st Lieut.	4th Regt. T.M.V.	
2. W. J. Thompson	2nd Lieut.	" " "	
3. F. A. Hill	" "	" " "	
4. A. Testard	" "	5th " "	
5. A. P. Goldsberry	" "	7th " "	

Orders were issued directing elections by the Companies to supply the vacancies so occasioned which were held in accordance therewith, and the vacancies have been thus supplied. These resignations should have been forwarded sooner, but the unavoidable hurry and confusion of preparation for the march from San Antonio caused me to overlook them.

I have the honor to be, General
Very respectfully your obt Servt.
(Signed)   A. M. Jackson
Ass. Adjt. Genl.
Army of New Mexico

79.

Hd. Qrs. Army of New Mexico A.G.O.
Fort Bliss Texas. Jany. 2nd 1861 [1862]

Major H. W. Raguet
Com^{dg} 4th Regt. T.M.V.

Major:

The General Commanding directs that you will advance with your Regt. without delay, as far as Fort Thorn, where you will go into camp.

Flour for your command is being sent forward from Hart's Mills in this vicinity. Other supplies will be forwarded as soon as possible.

I am, Major
your obt Servt.
(Signed)   A. M. Jackson
Ass. Adjt. Genl.
Army of New Mexico

80.

Hd. Qrs. Army of New Mexico A.G.O.
Fort Bliss Tex: Jany. 2nd 1862

General S. Cooper
Adjt. & Insp. Genl. C.S.A.

General.

I have the honor of enclosing to you a copy of a communication from Lt. Colonel Roberts U.S.A. commanding at Fort Craig N.M. to Col. Baylor at Messilla, proposing an exchange of prisoners, which communication was forwarded to me by Col. Baylor for my orders. A copy of my reply to Col. Baylor acceding to the proposition and directing that officer to effect it, is also enclosed.

For the future information of your office, I also enclose a copy of Lt. [William] Simmons' letter to Col. Baylor relative to his treatment by the U.S. Officers.

I have further to report that last evening Lt. Simmons reported to me at these Hd. Qrs., the exchange having been effected by which he was released.

I am Sir, very respectfully
your obt Servant
(Signed)   H. H. Sibley
Brig. Genl. P.A.C.S.
Commanding

81.

Hd. Qrs. Army of New Mexico A.G.O.
Fort Bliss Tex: Jany. 3rd 1862

General S. Cooper
Adjt. & Insp. Genl. C.S.A.
General:

I have the honor to report that in view of the importance of establishing satisfactory relations with the adjacent Mexican States of Chihuahua and Sonora, I have ordered Col. James Reily, 4th Regt. T.M.V. to proceed to the capitals of those States for the purpose of delivering to their respective Governors the communications which I have addressed to them, and of conferring which [with] those officials in person upon the subjects of those communications.

On the 21st day of Dec., I forwarded to you copies of the principal communication above alluded to. I have now the honor of enclosing copies of my letters accrediting Col. Reily to those functionaries, and also of my instructions to him in regard to the duties assigned him in this mission.

Col. Reily left these Head Quarters for the city of Chihuahua on yesterday, the 2nd instant. The result of this mission when known, will be promptly communicated to you.

> I have the honor, to be
> General
> Very respectfully
> your obt Servt.

(Signed)   H. H. Sibley
> Brig. Genl. P.A.C.S.
> Commanding[5]

82.

Hd. Qrs. Army of New Mexico A.G.O.
Fort Bliss Tex: Jany. 3rd 1862

General S. Cooper
Adjt. & Insp. Genl. C.S.A.
General:

On the 1st of Nov. 1861 I appointed W. S. Wood to be an Acting First Lieutenant in the Provisional Army, subject to the approval of the President, and assigned him to duties with the Field Artillery of the 5th Regt. (Col. Green's) T.M.V.

On the 2nd of the same month, I appointed Phillip Fulchrod [Philip Fulcrod] Acting Second Lieut. in the Provisional Army, subject to the approval of the President, and assigned him to duty with the same Corps.

My Asst. Adjt. General informs me that there is some doubt whether these appointments were communicated to you when made, as they should have been.

These appointments were made upon the urgent recommendations of Col. Green, who found that competent officers for his Artillery were not to be obtained by detail from among his subalterns.

Esteeming an efficient organization of this Arm very important, I fully concurred in Col. Green's recommendation of these appointments which I trust will meet the approbation of his Excellency.

In that case, I request that you will cause the commissions for those officers to bear date from their appointments as above (since when they have been on duty) to be forwarded to care of these Head Quarters.

I have the honor to be, General
Very respectfully your obt Servt.
(Signed)   H. H. Sibley
Brig. Genl. P.A.C.S.
Army of New Mexico

83.

Hd. Qrs. Army of New Mexico A.G.O.
Fort Bliss Tex. Jany. 3rd 1862

Major H. W. Raguet
Comdg 4th Regt. T.M.V.

Major:

The General Commanding directs me to inform you that four additional Wagons for your transportation are being sent to you with all possible despatch.

He also directs that you will detach your dismounted men, and those who are without arms in consequence of the transmission of their Arms to this point for repairs, and to send such men (dismounted and disarmed) under proper officers to this place, commissioned and non commissioned.

By supplying the unarmed men as far as practicable from the efficient arms of the dismounted men, you can probably materially reduce the number of men necessary to be left for those reasons.

The General Comdg directs that no delay in your advance should be allowed by reason of any deficiencies in the respects alluded to. He was not informed until today of the deficiencies in arms occasioned by the cause above referred to.

I am Major your obt Servt.
(Signed)   A. M. Jackson
Ass. Adjt. Genl.
Army of New Mexico

84.

Hd. Qrs. Army of New Mexico
Fort Bliss Tex: Jany. 3rd 1862

Colonel Thos. Green
Comdg 5th Regt. T.M.V.
Colonel:

The General Comdg directs that you will order Lt. Col. McNeill and the four Companies under his command, to take up the line of march for Fort Thorn, in the morning.

Two additional Wagons will be furnished for their transportation, on your requisition.

I am, Colonel
your obt Servt.
(Signed)   A. M. Jackson
Ass. Adjt. Genl.
Army of New Mexico

85.

Hd. Qrs. Army of New Mexico A.G.O.
Fort Bliss Tex: Jany. 3rd 1861 [1862]

Colonel Thos. Green
Comdg 5th Regt. T.M.V.
Colonel:

The Genl. Commanding directs that Sergeant W. J. Bullard, Corporal A. Wilkinson [sic], and Privates W. Hines, S. Nunn, J. S. Holbert, H. Whitner, J. C. Carter, and [E. P.] Carver, all of Captain Campbell's Company "G" [Company F], be detailed for duty with these Head Quarters. Sergeant Bullard as Orderly to the General, the others as expressmen, under the command of Sergt. Bullard.

You will please give the necessary orders upon this subject.

I am Colonel
your obt Servt.
(Signed)   A. M. Jackson
Ass. Adjt. Genl.
Army of New Mexico

COLONEL JOHN ROBERT BAYLOR
(Hill Memorial Library, Louisiana State University)

ALEXANDER M. JACKSON

Brigadier General Edward Richard Sprigg Canby

(Jerry Thompson)

Banner of the Sibley Brigade
(Henry C. Sibley Jr.)

86.

Hd. Qrs. Army of New Mexico A.G.O.
Fort Bliss Tex. Jany. 6th 1862

To Com[dg] Officer C.S.A.
Fort Fillmore

The General Commanding this Army, has had complaints made to him by Mr. Hugh Stevenson [Stephenson] the lessee or owner of Fort Fillmore, viz.; that certain persons not Soldiers of the Confederate Army, have been using and otherwise destroying the fuel belonging to said Stevenson in and about said Military Post.

These [orders] are to command you to use every exertion to stop the same, and if necessary the General Commanding orders you to furnish such assistance to Mr. Stevenson as he may require to suppress the same.

By orders of Brig. Genl.
H. H. Sibley
(Signed)   Tom P. Ochiltree
Aid de Camp to Genl. Sibley
Army of N.M.

87.

Hd. Qrs. Army of New Mexico
Fort Bliss Tex. Jany. 10th 1862

General S. Cooper
Adjt. & Insp. Genl. C.S.A.

General:

I have the honor herewith to enclose the proceedings of a Military Commission convened by General Orders No. 1 present series, from these Hd. Qrs.

I have the honor to be
Very respectfully your obt Servt.
(Signed)   Tom P. Ochiltree
A.D.C. & Act. A.A.G.
Army of New Mexico

88.

Hd. Qrs. Army of New Mexico
Fort Thorn Ar. Jany. 20th 1862

Commanding Officer
Fort Bliss Texas
    Sir.
The Com^{dg} General directs that you will detach a party of
footmen belonging to the 1st Regt. T.M.V. from your Post with
orders to march to this point. Let them be armed with the Guns in
the hands of the Ordnance Dept. for repairs, and supply them
with the necessary ammunition.

Instruct the officer or non com. officer in command to march
with the supply train of subsistence and give it protection jointly
with the escort already detailed for that purpose.

Very respectfully
your obt Servt.
(Signed)   Tom P. Ochiltree
A.D.C. to Genl. Sibley

89.

Hd. Qrs. Army of New Mexico
Fort Thorn Ar. Jany. 20th 62

To Commanding Officer
Fort Bliss Texas
    Sir.
The General Comm^{dg} directs that you will without
unnecessary delay forward by wagon to this place, the Three
Mountain Howitzers 'complete' now at Fort Bliss, and also 100
rounds of ammunition for the same.

Very respectfully
your obt Servt.
(Signed) Tom P. Ochiltree
A.D.C. to Genl. Sibley

90.

Hd. Qrs. Army of New Mexico A.G.O.
Fort Thorn Ar. Jany. 22nd 1862

Col. J. R. Baylor
Comdg at Mesilla Ar.
Colonel.

Yours of 21st inst., covering a petition by men of Captain Coopwood's Company has been received. The General will give their request a further consideration, and you will be advised of his conclusion in reference thereto.

Enclosed I forward you the appointment of Adjutant [Michael] Looscue [Looscan] made upon your recommendation.

I am Colonel
your obt Servt.
(Signed)   A. M. Jackson
Ass. Adjt. Genl.
Army of New Mexico

91.

Hd. Qrs. Army of New Mexico
Fort Thorn Ar. Jany. 22. 62

Col. J. R. Baylor
Com^{dg} at Mesilla Ar.
Colonel.

In reply to yours of the 21st inst., reporting the arrest of John Lemmons [Lemon] and his party, I am directed by the Genl. Com^{dg} to state that he presumes that this is the same person and party whom he had employed for scout service in New Mexico, in the distribution of his Proclamation. If so, his arrest is possibly made under a misapprehension and you are directed to enquire particularly into the matter and the circumstances attending Mr. Lemmon's departure. You will report the result of such enquiry, and retain the prisoners until further orders. Mr. Jno. Phillips is cognizant of the arrangement between the General and Mr. Lemmons, and may be able to throw light in the matter.

I am Colonel
your obt Servt.
(Signed)   A. M. Jackson
Ass. Adjt. Genl.
Army of N.M.

92.

Hd. Qrs. Army of New Mexico A.G.O.
Fort Thorn Ar. Jany. 22. 62

Col. J. R. Baylor
Com^{dg} at Mesilla Ar.
Colonel.

Your communication applying for orders to Captain Hunter to move with his Company to Tucson, for service there and to facilitate recruiting for your Regiment in Southern California, has been submitted to the General Commanding.

I am instructed by him to reply that he is not now prepared to determine in regard to it, but will do so upon further consideration and advise you further at an early day.

1 am Colonel
your obt Servt.
(Signed)   A. M. Jackson
Ass. Adjt. Genl.
Army of New Mexico

93.

Hd. Qrs., Army of New Mexico
Fort Thorn, Ar, Jan. 22, 62

Col. J. R. Baylor
Comdg at Mesilla, Ar
Colonel:

In compliance with your recommendation the Genl Comdg authorizes the sale of [*sic*] the men of your command of the Government horses heretofore distributed among them. You will see that proper steps are taken to protect the interest of the Government by valuations made by disinterested persons under your direction.

I am Colonel
Your obt. Svt.
A. M. Jackson
A. Adjt. Genl
Army of N.M.

94.

Hd. Qrs. Army of New Mexico A.G.O.
Fort Thorn, N.M. Jany. 23rd 1862

Col. J. R. Baylor
Com^{dg} at Mesilla Ar.

Colonel:

The Genl. Commanding directs that, with as little delay as practicable, you will advance the whole of your available force to this place. He particularly desires that Capt. Teel's Company of Artillery shall report with full ranks and in as efficient condition for active service at an early day. Energy and promptitude are enjoined in this movement.

You will transfer the command and civil authority to such officers as you shall select.

I am Colonel
your obt Servt.
(Signed)   A. M. Jackson
Asst. Adjt. Genl.
Army of N.M.

95.

Hd. Qrs. Army of New Mex.
Fort Thorn Ar. Jany. 27. 62

Col. James Reily
4th Regt. T.M.V.
Colonel:

Your report and accompanying documents touching your mission to the Government of Chihuahua, were received by the Genl. Comdg, and are in all respects satisfactory. They will be communicated from these Head Quarters to the Government at Richmond.

The Genl. now directs that you will proceed to Sonora, so soon as the necessary arrangements can be effected. In respect to the funds required the Genl. considers the arrangements already made with Judge Hart as still subsisting. Col. Baylor is ordered, by communication direct to him, to detach Captain Hunter and his Company for service in Western Arizona, and incidentally to afford you by this detachment protection to some point at or beyond the frontier of Sonora where other protection can be procured. You will communicate with Col. Baylor or the officer in command at Mesilla in regard to the time at which Captain Hunter can be ready to move.

No further instruction than those heretofore furnished you, relative to the purposes of your mission, are deemed necessary.

> I am Colonel
> your obt Servt
> (Signed)   A. M. Jackson
> Ass. Adjt. Genl.
> Army of N.M.

96.

Hd. Qrs. Army of New Mexico
Fort Thorn Ar. Jany. 27. 62

Col. J. R. Baylor
Com^{dg} at Mesilla
Colonel.

In accordance with your request contained in your communication of the 19th inst., the Genl. Com^{dg} directs that you will detach Captain Hunter and his Company for service in Western Arizona, to be stationed at Tucson.

Col. James Reily 4th Regt. T.M.V. is under orders to proceed to Sonora upon public business and the General desires that Captain Hunter shall escort him and his party to the frontier of that State, or to some point beyond it where Col. Reily can obtain other protection. You will give Captain Hunter the necessary orders to this end. All arrangements for the transportation and subsistence of Capt. Hunter's command will be made by you.

I am Col.
your obt Servt.
(Signed)   A. M. Jackson
Ass. Adjt. Genl.
Army of N.M.

97.

Hd. Qrs. Army of New Mexico
Fort Thorn Ar. Jany. 28th 62

Genl. S. Cooper
Adjt. & Insp. Genl. C.S.A.

General:

I have the honor to inform you that I am in receipt of a report from Col. James Reily of his mission to the Governor of Chihuahua, of which you have been heretofore advised. For your information I enclose the original documents, consisting of the report of Col. Reily, and the communications to him and to myself of the Governor of that State, touching the various matters brought by me to the attention of that ~~Governor~~ Official by communications of which copies were duly forwarded to you.

The Governor's communication will, I think, be considered important and highly satisfactory.

By orders of this date, Col. Reily is directed to proceed to the State of Sonora on a similar mission, which I hope will prove equally successful.

I have the honor to be
General
your obt Servt.
(Signed)   H. H. Sibley
Brig. Genl.
Commanding

P.S. With a view to the protection of the important and growing interest, chiefly mineral, in W. Arizona, and for the further purpose of opening communications with Southern California whose people are favorably inclined to our government, I have ordered one Company (Capt. Hunter's) of Col. Baylor's command to take post at Tucson.

Respectfully
H.H.S.[6]

98.

Hd. Qrs. Army of New Mexico
Fort Thorn Ar. Jany. 28th 62

Col. J. R. Baylor
Com^{dg} at Mesilla
Colonel.

In view of the detachment of Capt. Hunter's Company for service in Western Arizona and the requirements of the public service in reference to the supplies for that Company, and in consideration of the necessities which exist or may arise for the superintendence of some superior officer over military and civil affairs in Arizona, the General Com^{dg} now directs that you will continue in command and in the exercise of the Gubernatorial powers of that Territory, and will forward your available forces under command of their respective officers, if there is no other field officer for duty.

I am Colonel
your obt Servt.
(Signed)   A. M. Jackson
Ass. Adjt. Genl.
Army of N.M.

99.

Hd. Qrs. Army of New Mexico
Fort Thorn Ar. Jany. 28th 62

Major R. C. Myers [Lt. Col. Abraham C. Myers]
Qr. Master Genl. C.S.A.

Colonel:

I am in receipt of your communication of Dec. 26th 61, relative to certain mule teams pertaining to the Qr. Master's service of the Dept. of Texas taken by Col. Reily 4th Regt. T.M.V. while en route for El Paso from San Antonio, with his command. My Brig. Qr. Master, Capt. W. H. Harrison had previously reported to these Hd. Qrs. that he had receipted to Maj. [J. F.] Minter for this property which I presume places the matter right so far as Maj. M. is concerned, who should, it seems to me, have reported this fact to you.

I am Col.
your obt Servt.
(Signed)   H. H. Sibley
Brig. Genl.
Commanding

100.

Hd. Qrs. Army of New Mexico
Fort Thorn Ar. Jany. 28. 62

Maj. R. H. Chilton
Ass. Adjt. Genl. C.S.A.
Sir.

Your communication of the 28th Dec. 61, requesting a list of the Officers and Men captured by Col. J. R. Baylor in the Territory of Arizona, was this day received.

Col. Baylor, who is now at Mesilla, has been ordered to forward you the list called for.

I am, Sir
your obt Servt.
(Signed)   A. M. Jackson
Ass. Adjt. Genl.
Army of N.M.

101.

Hd. Qrs. Army of New Mexico
Fort Thorn Ar. Jany. 28th 62

General S. Cooper
Adjt. & Insp. Genl. C.S.A.
General.

I have the honor to communicate that on the 22nd inst., I appointed subject to the approval of his Excellency the President, Mr. Looscan to be Adjutant with the rank of 1st Lt., to the Regt. of Mt. Vol's to be raised by Col. J. R. Baylor.

On the 26th inst., subject to the President's approval, I appointed J. H. Beck (late 2nd Lt. 5th Regt. T.M.V.) to be Com. of Sub. of said Regt. (5th T.M.V. Col. Thos. Green) with the rank of Captain.

On the 12th inst. I appointed J. M. Noble (1st Lieut. 4th Regt. T.M.V.) to be Commissary of Subsistence of that Regiment (4th T.M.V.) with the rank of Captain.

All those appointments were made upon the recommendations of the Commanding Officers of the Regiments designated. The commissions for the officers should, if their appointments are confirmed, bear date from the days of their appointments by me, at which dates they went upon duty. That for Adjutant Looscan should be directed to La Mesilla, Arizona. The other two to these Head Quarters.

> I have the honor to be
> General
> your obt Servt.
> (Signed)   H. H. Sibley
> Commanding

102.

Hd. Qrs. Army of New Mexico
Fort Thorn Ar. Jany. 28. 62

General S. Cooper
Adjt. & Insp. Genl. C.S.A.
General:

On the 7th of Nov. 1861, 1 had the honor of addressing you a communication relative to the Ordnance Service of the Brigade under my ~~Brigade~~ command, and recommending that an appointment as ordnance officer with such rank as the Dept. deemed appropriate should be conferred upon Mr. Willis L. Robards, who then was and still is the Acting Ordnance Officer of this Army. I beg that you will refer to that communication for the various reasons given for the recommendation. To this date no reply has been received, and in the meantime this gentleman has been most assiduously and most efficiently engaged in the difficult and vexatious duties of that position.

I feel that justice to him requires me to urge again this matter upon your attention, and to ask that if my request for his appointment in the Ord. Dept. is not deemed admissible, that some other Staff appointment, placing him in a proper official and responsible position should be assigned him.

I have the honor to be
General
your obt Servt.

(Signed)   H. H. Sibley
Brig. Genl.
Commanding

103.

Hd. Qrs. Army of New Mexico
Fort Thorn Az. Jany. 28. 62

Col. J. R. Baylor
Com^{dg} at Mesilla

Colonel:

Charges have been placed on file here against Lt. [Jesse H.] Holden of your command and Pvt. Graftrath [Jacob Graffrath] of Capt. Teel's Company also of your command. They are of a nature requiring a Genl. Court Martial. You will cause the prisoners and witnesses to be forwarded here at once when such a court will be organized for their trial. The Companies of your command being under orders for this place, it is not believed practicable to organize the Court elsewhere than here. But if the prisoners and witnesses cannot be sent up during this week, let the cases stand over, as the contemplated advance of this Army may not permit of the organization of a Court at a later day.

I am Colonel
your obt Servt.
(Signed)   A. M. Jackson
Ass. Adjt. Genl.
Army of N.M.

104.

Hd. Qrs. Army of New Mexico
Fort Thorn Ar. Jany. 30th 62

J. R. Baylor
Col. Com^{dg} at Mesilla
    Colonel:
    The Genl. Com^{dg} understands from Capt. [Isaac C.] Stafford
that there are a considerable number of effective guns, belonging
to the sick of your command and otherwise on hand in Mesilla and
your other posts, which can be spared for a time from your troops
without prejudice. In view of the very great difficiencies [*sic*] in
arms existing among the other troops, he directs that you will
cause those guns, and also all six shooting pistols not needed for
immediate service, to be forwarded here by the transportation sent
by the Qr. Master. Capt. Stafford goes down to give his personal
attention to this matter. Proper invoices should of course be taken,
so that the Arms can be identified hereafter.

I am Colonel
your obt Servt.
(Signed)   A. M. Jackson
Ass. Adjt. Genl.
Army of N.M.

105.

Hd. Qrs. Army of New Mexico
Fort Thorn Ar. Feby. 5th 62

Col. J. R. Baylor
Com^{dg} at Mesilla

Colonel:

Three persons named Kirk, Kennedy, and Lance have been arrested here by order of the General Com^{dg}, upon the charge of stealing and carrying off to Chihuahua a train of public property of the United States, some months since, and selling the same there for their own benefit.

The General is informed that these persons or some of them now have a portion of the proceeds of this property (amt^g to $6000.00/100 or more) on deposit at Franklin with Mss. Richardson & Knox or some other parties there.

The General directs that you will make particular enquiry into the fact of this deposit, and if you find it to be true, you will demand and require such funds to be delivered to you for the benefit of the Confederate States, giving all proper receipts for the same exhibiting the authority by which you make such seizure.

I am Colonel
your obt Servt.

(Signed)   A. M. Jackson
Ass. Adjt. Genl.
Army of New Mexico

106.

Hd. Qrs. Army of New Mexico
Fort Thorn Ar. Feby. 6th 62

Ass. Surg. E. N. Covey C.S.A.
Med. Dir. & Purveyor
Army of New Mex.
    Sir:
    The General Commanding directs that you will at once
proceed to rejoin these Hd. Qrs. for duty. This order being
directed in anticipation of an immediate advance of this Army,
you will appreciate the necessity of a prompt compliance.

I am Sir
your obt Servt.
(Signed)   A. M. Jackson
Ass. Adjt. Genl.
Army of N.M.

107.

Hd. Qrs. Army of New Mexico A.G.O.
Fort Thorn Ar. Feby. 6th 1862

To Col. Baylor at Mesilla or
Lieut. Taylor en route or
Capt. S. Hunter at Doña Ana
    The General Com^{dg} directs that the men Kirk and Lance who
were arrested here and sent down by Lieut. Taylor this morning
and the man Kennedy who is ordered to be arrested at Doña Ana,
shall be sent back here by the party who takes down this dispatch.
    All Officers to whom this order is addressed will see to it that
it shall be complied with, at once.
    If Kennedy is not arrested as yet, officers below will exert
themselves to cause his arrest and send him up. In the meantime
the others will be forwarded by the party conveying this dispatch.

[no signature block]

108.

Hd. Qrs. Army of New Mexico

Fort Thorn Ar. Feby. 7th 62

To the Commanding Officer U.S. Forces

    at Fort Craig N.M.

        Sir:

        Within the last two days I have been enabled to arrest certain persons named Kirk and Lance, who were notoriously concerned in the theft and embezzlement of a supply train of the U.S. in April of the past year. Although the offense is one which might be punishable here under the Martial Law existing by my authority, yet as the crime was one more directly affecting the U.S. it appears to me to be more conformable to the principles of right and of courtesy which should be regarded among civilized people even in times of War, to turn these malefactors over to the government of the U.S. for its disposition of them. Accordingly they are forwarded to you by the command which conveys them.

    A deposition of the man Lance, taken by my order relative to the theft and disposition of the property is enclosed herewith.

    The course I thus pursue in the transfer of these men to your jurisdiction, is taken in conformity with the established policy of my government to repress crime by every means available to its authorities.

    I further state that there are others who were implicated in the theft, whose names I have. So soon as I can effect their apprehension, they also will be sent forward to you.

I am Sir, with proper

consideration

(Signed)   H. H. Sibley

                Brig. General C.S.A.

                Commanding Army N.M.

109.

Hd. Qrs. Army of New Mexico A.G.O.
Fort Thorn Ar. Feby. 7th 1862

To the Commanding Officer of U.S. Forces
    at Fort Craig
        Sir:
        I desire hereby to accredit to you as bearers of a Flag of Truce for the purpose of delivering to you a communication from me, my Aids de Camp, Col. W. L. Robards and Capt. J. E. Dwyer.

I bespeak for these gentlemen all the courtesies and attention to which they are entitled in their private as well as their official character, and I beg leave to commend them to you as in every respect worthy of your esteem and consideration.

I am Sir your Friend & obt Servt.
(Signed)   H. H. Sibley
Brig. Genl. Commanding
Army of N.M.

110.

Hd. Qrs. Army of New Mexico
Fort Thorn Ar. Feby. 9th 62

Col. James Reily
4th Regt. T.M.V.
Colonel.

In reply to your recommendations and requests heretofore communicated to these Head Quarters, I am authorized by the Genl. Com^{dg} to state.

First. That for your expenditures of all kinds, you are authorized to draw upon the Qr. Master of this Army for the sum of Two Thousand Dollars. Of course you must make your own arrangements for the negotiations of such drafts, if found necessary before you can obtain the funds in Treasury notes from the Q.M., who has them subject to your drafts.

Second. If you should, upon further observation and full reflection, still be of the opinion that an extension of your mission to the City of Mexico, would be promotive of the interest of the Confederacy, you are authorized so to extend it. It is likely, however, that the President at Richmond may be better able to judge of the proper time to inaugurate a public mission to the Federal Government of Mexico than anyone on this frontier can possibly be.

Third. Your powers to treat with the Pimos, Papagos, and other tribes of the Pueblo or other friendly-disposed Indians are ample and full so far as it is within the competency of the General to confer them, and your suggestions in regard thereto are highly approved.

I am, Colonel
your obt Servt.
(Signed)   A. M. Jackson
Ass. Adjt. Genl. P.C.S.A.
Army of N.M.

111.

Hd. Qrs. Army of New Mexico
Valverde, N.M. Feby. 21, 1862

Col. E. Canby
Com^{dg} U.S. Forces in the
    Territory of New Mexico
    Colonel:

I desire hereby to accredit to you Lieut. Col. Wm R. Scurry of the 4th and Capt. D. W. Shannon of the 5th Regiment of Texas Mt. Vol's in the service of the Confederate States. These gentlemen are dispatched under flag of Truce to hold communication with you upon matters pertaining to the Military Service of our respective Governments, in regard to which they will express to you my views and purposes.

I commend them as officers and gentlemen to your highest esteem and confidence.

I am, Colonel
your obt. Servt.
(Signed)   H. H. Sibley
Brig. Genl. Army of Conf. States
Com^{dg} Army of New Mexico[7]

112.

Hd. Qrs. Army of New Mexico
Albuquerque N.M. Mch. 10, 1862

To the Commanding Officer of
The United States Forces at
Fort Union, N.M.

Sir:

I hereby accredit to you as Bearer of a Flag of Truce, Lieut. Col. H. C. McNeill 5th Regt. Texas Mtd. Vols., who proceeds by my orders to propose to you an exchange of prisoners.

I am informed that you hold as prisoners of War, Lt. Nicholson and four privates, of this Army, and that you retain for political causes certain Southern citizens, the particular nature of whose offences has not reached me in any official form.

We hold as prisoners of War, at this place, Lieut. Tester, Dr. Gray, Sergt. Brown and private Custis, besides many heretofore released upon parole but who are still, of course, subject to exchange.

Lieut. Col. McNeill is fully empowered to conclude a general exchange, grade for grade, and to include in it our citizens said to be detained by you.

I am, Sir
your obt Servt.
(Signed)   H. H. Sibley
Brig. Genl. C.S.A. Comdg
Army of New Mexico

113.

Hd. Qrs. Army of New Mexico
Albuquerque N.M. Mch. 11th 1862

Don Lorenzo Montaño
Alguacil Mayor del
    Condado de Bernalillo
Sir:
    You are required to report yourself with your books and papers concerning Licenses and public Revenues, at these Head Quarters, without delay. You will bring with you all funds pertaining to the Territorial Treasury.

By order of Brig. Genl.
H. H. Sibley

Ass. Adjt. Genl.
Army of New Mexico

114.

Hd. Qrs. Army of New Mex.
Alb: N.M. Mch. 25th 1862

Colonel:

A concentration of forces of this Army at some ~~point~~ strategic or commanding position, is desired at an early day. The General directs that you immediately occupy Mansana [Manzano] for that purpose.

It is also desired that a Depot for supplies be established at Mansana for ulterior operations. You will take the necessary steps for the accomplishment of this object.

The General Comdg requests that as far as in your power lies, you will prepare for the accommodation of the Corps of this Army as they arrive.

I have the honor to be
Very respectfully your
obt Servt.
(Signed)   Tom P. Ochiltree
Asst. Adjt. Genl

To
Col. W. R. Scurry
Army of N.M.
Comdg 4th & 7th Regt.
T.M.V.

115.

Head Quarters, Army of New Mexico A.G.O.
Albuquerque, N.M. March 27, 1862

Captain.

Upon the receipt of this communication you will at once take up the line of march for this point, with your command, evacuating Covero [Cubero] and bringing under your protection and escort all the ammunition and such other supplies as can be transported with the means at your disposal.

Some few wagons were dispatched from here for the ammunition, a few days ago. It is expected they will reach you in time to return with you bringing supplies. Any other means of transportation which you can obtain without delaying your movements you are authorized and directed to procure.

I am, Captain
Your obdt. Servt.

(Signed) A. M. Jackson

Capt. [Alfred S.] Thurmond   Asst. Adjt. Genl.
Com^{dg} at Covero   Army of New Mexico

P.S. Supplies and munitions of war, beyond your means of removing, you will dispose of so as to put them beyond the reach of the enemy should he at any time reoccupy Covero. Buildings are not to be injured or destroyed.

116.

Head Quarters, Army of New Mex.
Fort Bliss, Texas. May 4th 1862

Genl. S. Cooper
Adjutant & Inspector Genl.
    Richmond Va.
        General.
            I have the honor to report for the information of
the Secretary of War, the operations of this Army during the
months of February, March & April Ultimo. This report is made to
cover the whole campaign, for the reasons that the special reports
of the various commanders, herewith enclosed, enter sufficiently
into detail to elucidate the various actions, in which the troops
were engaged during the campaign.

It is due to the brave soldiers I have had the honor to
command, to premise, that from its first inception the "Sibley
Brigade" has encountered difficulties in its organization and
opposition and distaste to the service required at its hands, which
no other troops have met with.

From misunderstandings, accidents, deficiency of arms,
clothing, etc. instead of reaching the field of operations early in
September as was anticipated, I found myself at this point as late as
the month of January '62 with only two Regts. and a half, poorly
~~mounted~~ armed, thinly clad, and almost destitute of blankets. The
ranks were becoming daily thinned, with those terrible scourges to
an army: Small pox and Pneumonia.

Not a dollar of Quartermaster funds were on hand or had ever
been [sent?] to supply the daily and pressing necessities of the
service, and the small means of this sparse section had been long
consumed by the force under the command of Lieut. Col. Jno. R.
Baylor, so that the credit of the government was not as available as
it otherwise might have been.

Having established a General Hospital at Doña Ana, I
determined to move forward with the force at hand. Accordingly

during the first week in January, the advance was put on march for old Fort Thorn. Thence on the 7th of February the movement was continued without interruption to a point seven miles below Fort Craig, where the Santa Fe papers boasted, we were to be met and overwhelmed by Canby's entire army. On the 16th of February a reconnaissance in force was pushed to within a mile of the Fort, and battle offered in the open plain. The challenge was disregarded and only noticed by the sending out [of] a few well mounted men to watch our movements. The forces of the enemy were left carefully concealed in the "Bosque" above the Fort and within its walls.

This reconnaissance proved the futility of assaulting ~~the Fort~~ in front with our light mettle [metal], and that our only hope of success was to force the enemy to an open-field fight. It was accordingly determined, by a partial retrograde movement, to cross the Rio Grande to the east bank, turn the Fort and force a battle for the recrossing. To do this, involved first, the hazardous necessity of crossing a treacherous stream in full view of the Fort. Second, to make a dry camp immediately opposite and remote only a mile and a half, and the next day to fight our first battle.

The enemy seemed to have been so confounded by the boldness and eccentricity of these movements that the first were accomplished without molestation, save a demonstration on the afternoon of the 20th as we were forming our camp, by the crossing of some 2500 Infantry and Cavalry with the purpose apparently of making an assault upon our lines. Here the spirit and high courage of our men were evident by the alacrity shown in getting into line to confront the enemy. A few rounds from our well-directed guns, under the management of Capt. Teel, Lieuts. Reily and Wood, checked his advance and drove him to the cover of sand [-revetted] mud walls.

It is proper to state here, that these operations approved by me, were conducted by Col. Thos. Green of the 5th Regt., the state of my health having confined me to the ambulance for several days previous.

On the morning of the 21st considering that the impending battle must decide the question at issue, though very weak I took the saddle at early dawn to direct in person the movements. Green's Regt. with the Battalion of the 7th under Lt. Col. Sutton and Capt. Teel's Battery, were ordered to make a strong threatening demonstration upon the Fort, whilst Scurry with the 4th well flanked by Pyron's Command on the left, should feel his way cautiously to the River.

This movement was unfortunately delayed by the loss during the night, by careless herding, of a hundred mules of the baggage train of the 4th Regt. Rather than the plan should be defeated, a number of wagons were abandoned, containing the entire Kits, blankets, books & papers of this Regt. Meanwhile, what was left of the trains was put in motion over the sand hills which the enemy had deemed impassable. On reaching the river bottom at Valverde, it was ascertained that the enemy anticipating our movement had thrown a large force of Infantry and Cavalry up the river to dispute the water with us.

Pyron immediately engaged him with his small force of 250 men and gallantly held his ground against overwhelming odds, until the arrival of Scurry with the 4th & Lt. Reily's Battery of light Howitzers. At 12 N. the action becoming warm and the enemy evidently receiving large reinforcements, I ordered Green's Regt. with Teel's Battery to the front. These in the course of an hour gallantly entered into action, and the battle became general. Subsequently, Lieut. Col. Sutton with his battalion was ordered forward from the rear, and did right good service boldly leading his men even to the cannon's mouth.

At 1½ P.M. having become completely exhausted and finding myself no longer able to keep the saddle, I sent my aids and other staff officers to report to Col. Green. His official report attests the gallantry of their bearing and his final success, resulting in the capture of their battery and driving the enemy in disorder from the field, is sufficient evidence of his own intrepidity and of the indomitable courage of all engaged. From information derived from reliable sources the force immediately opposed to us could not have been less than 5000 with a reserve of 3000 at the Fort. Ours did not exceed 1750 on the field, viz.; the 4th 600, 7th 300, 5th 600, Pyron's 250.

This signal victory should have resulted in the capture of the Fort, as fresh troops had been brought forward to pursue and follow his discomfited columns. A flag of truce, opportunely dispatched by the Federal Commander before he reached the gates of the Fort, and which for two hours was supposed by our troops to be a proposition to surrender, stopped all further operations, night having meanwhile intervened. Their flag had for its object the burying of their dead and taking off the wounded, and I regret to state here for the sake of old associations that under this flag and another sent the next day, the enemy availing himself of our generosity and confidence in his honor, not only loaded his wagons with arms picked up on the battle field, but sent a force up and actually succeeded in recovering from the river one twenty-four pounder which had virtually been left in our hands. Even a flag and a guidon taken in the same way, under the cover of night and a white flag, were boastingly pointed to in an interview under a flag of truce between one of my aids and the Federal Commander at the Fort as trophies of the fight.

The burying of the dead and care of our wounded, occasioned a delay of two days on the field, thus leaving us with but five days' scant rations. In this dilemma, the question arose whether to assault the Fort in this crippled condition or move rapidly forward up the river where supplies of bread stuffs and meat could be procured. The latter course in a council of war, was adopted. Depositing our sick at Socorro, thirty miles above Fort Craig, the march was uninterruptedly made to Albuquerque where, notwithstanding the destruction of large supplies by fire, ample subsistence was secured at that point, at Cubero, a town sixty miles west, and at Santa Fé [sic] for three months.

It is due to the 4th Regiment to mention at this place an act of devotion and self-sacrifice, worthy of high praise and the more

commendable, because they are Texans. In the action many of
their horses were killed, thus leaving them half foot, half
dragoons. The proposition was made to them to dismount the
entire Regiment. Without a dissenting voice, a Cavalry Regiment,
which had proudly flaunted its banners before the enemy on the
20th, took the line of march on the 24th, a strong and reliable Regt.
of Infantry.

Having secured all the available stores in and about
Albuquerque and dispatched Major Pyron with his command to
Santa Fé, to secure such as might be found there, I determined to
make a strong demonstration on Fort Union. With this view, Scurry
with the 4th and the battalion of Steele's Regt. under Major Jordan
was pushed forward in the direction of Galisteo, whilst Green with
his Regt. (5th) somewhat crippled in transportation, was held for a
few days in hand to check any movement from Craig.

Meanwhile, the enemy having received reinforcement at Fort
Union of 950 men from Pike's Peak on [or about March 12] took
the initiative and commenced a rapid march on Santa Fé. Major
Shropshire, Major Pyron, reinforced by four companies of the 5th
receiving notice of this movement, advanced at once to meet him
on the high road on the [26th]. A sharp skirmish ensued, described
in detail by that Officer, wherein many acts of daring heroism are
detailed as having been enacted.

The company of "Brigands" under the command of Capt.
John Phillips is reported to have done good service, one of their
number [Mr. Thomas Cator] having been killed and two
wounded. On this occasion as on every previous one they have
shown a devotedness to the cause which has elevated them and
inspired confidence in the *fraternity* throughout the Army.

Col. Scurry reached the scene of action at daylight next
morning and the next day fought the battle of Glorietta, driving
the enemy from the field with great loss. His report is respectfully
referred to for the details of this glorious action.

Pending this battle I was on my route to Santa Fé in rear of
Green's Regt. which had meanwhile been put in march for that

city and when on my arrival, I found the whole exultant army assembled. The sick and wounded had been comfortably quartered and provided, the loss of clothing and transportation had been made up from the enemy's stores and confiscations, and, indeed, everything done which should have been done. Many friends were found in Santa Fé, who had been in durance. Among the rest, Genl. Pelham, who had but recently been released from a dungeon at Fort Union.

After the occupation of the Capital for [blank] days, the forage and supplies having become exhausted it was determined to occupy with the whole army the Village of Manzana, intermediate between Fort Union, Albuquerque and Fort Craig, and securing as a line of retreat the road to Fort Stanton. This plan was interrupted however by the rapid and continuous expresses from Albuquerque, urging the necessity of reinforcement to hold the place (the depot of all our supplies) against the advancing forces under Canby from Craig. The entire force was accordingly moved by forced marches in the direction of Albuquerque, arriving too late to encounter the enemy, but time enough to secure our limited supplies from the eventuality of capture.

In our straitened circumstances, the question now arose in my mind whether to evacuate the country or take the desperate chances of fighting the enemy in his stronghold—Union—for scant rations at the best. The course adopted was deemed the wisest.

On the morning of [April 12] the evacuation commenced by the crossing of Scurry's 4th Regiment, the battalion of Steele's Regt., Pyron's Command and part of the Artillery by ferry and by ford to the west bank of the river. Green's 5th Regiment was ordered to follow but finding the crossing worn and difficult, camped for the night on the east bank, and the next morning hoping to find a better ford lower down, that officer proceeded as low down as Peralta opposite Los Lunas, the point at which I had halted the balance of the command to await his arrival.

Meanwhile, Canby having formed a junction with a large force from Fort Union, debouched through a cañon, after night fall, on the river taking a commanding position in close proximity to Green's camp, and in the morning opened a furious but harmless cannonade. On being notified of the critical situation of this detached portion of the Army, the whole disposable force at Los Lunas, reserving a sufficient guard for the train, was dispatched to its relief. The crossing of the river by this force and the Artillery was successfully effected under the direction of Col. Scurry.

Following shortly after with a portion of my staff to assume the immediate command and having crossed the river, I was notified by several officers who had preceded me some hundred yards of the rapid approach of a large force of the enemy's cavalry. Finding myself completely cut off, I had no other alternative than to recross the river amid a shower of balls. The day was occupied in ineffectual firing on both sides. After nightfall I gave orders for the recrossing of the whole Army, which was effected without interruption or casualty, and the march down the river resumed next morning, followed by the enemy on the opposite bank, both Armies encamping in full view, the river alone intervening.

The transportation and Artillery had by this time become such an encumbrance on the heavy, sandy, road, without forage or grass, that the abandonment of one or the other became inevitable. My original plan had been to push on by the river route in advance of the enemy (having the start of him two whole days from Albuquerque) to Fort Craig, attack the weak garrison and demolish the Fort. This plan was defeated by the detention occasioned by Col. Green not finding a crossing of the river at a convenient point.

Col. Scurry, together with several other practical officers have come forward and proposed in order to avoid the contingency of another general action in our then crippled and embarrassed condition, that a route through the mountains, avoiding Fort Craig and striking the river below that point, and believed to be practicable, should be pursued, they undertaking with their respective commands to push the artillery through at all hazard and at any expenditure of toil and labor. Major Coopwood who had familiarized himself with the country undertook the difficult and responsible task of guiding the Army through the mountainous, trackless waste. The arguments presented in favor of this route were potent. Besides having the advantage of grass and a firm road with very little difference in distance, the enemy would be completely mystified as afterwards proved to be the case.

Accordingly all the wagons that could be possibly disposed with, were ordered to be abandoned on the ground, seven days' provisions to be packed on mules, and the entire force put in march after night fall. The route was a difficult and most hazardous one, both in respect to its practicability and supply of water. The successful accomplishment of the march has not only proved the sagacity of our guide, but the pledge of Col. Scurry that the Guns should be put over every obstacle by his Regiment (however formidable) was nobly fulfilled. Not a murmur escaped the lips of these brave boys. Descents into, and ascents out of the deepest cañons, while [sic] a single horseman would have sought for miles to avoid, were undertaken and accomplished with a cheerfulness and alacrity, which were the admiration and praise of the whole Army.

Thus in ten days, with seven days' rations, a point on the river, where supplies had been ordered forward, was reached. The river, which was rising rapidly, was safely crossed to the east bank under the direction of Col. Green, and at this moment I am happy to report, the whole force is comfortably quartered in the villages extending from Doña Ana to this place.

My chief regret in making this retrograde movement was the necessity of leaving Hospitals at Santa Fé, Albuquerque and Socorro. Everything however was provided for the comfort of the sick and sufficient funds in Confederate paper, to meet every want, provided it can be negotiated. It has been almost impossible to procure specie on any terms. One thousand dollars is all I have been able to attain for the use of the Hospitals and for secret service. The Ricos or wealthy citizens of New Mexico had been completely drained by the Federal Government, and adhered to it, and became absolute followers of the Army for dear life and their invested dollars. Politically they have no distinct sentiment or opinion on the vital question at issue. Power and interest alone controls the expression of their sympathies.

One noble and notable exception to their rule was found in the brothers Armijo, Manuel and Rafael, the wealthiest and most respectable merchants of New Mexico. The latter had been pressed into militia and had been in action at Valverde. On our arrival at Albuquerque they came forward boldly and protested their sympathy for our cause, and placed his entire house, containing goods amounting to 200,000 at the disposition of my troops. When the necessity for evacuating the country became inevitable, these two gentlemen abandoned luxurious homes and well-filled storehouses to join their fate to the Southern Confederacy. I trust they will not be forgotten in the final settlement.

In concluding this report, already extended beyond my anticipations, it is proper that I should express the conviction, determined by some experience that, except for its political geographical position, the Territory of New Mexico is not worth a quarter of the blood and treasure expended in its conquest. As a field for military operation it possesses not a single element except in the multiplicity of its defensible positions. The indispensable element food can not be relied upon. During the last year and pending the recent operation hundreds of thousands [of] sheep have been driven off by the Navajos. Indeed such were the complaints of the people in this respect, that I have determined as good policy to encourage private enterprises against that tribe and the Apaches and legitimize the making slaves of them.

As for the assults [*sic*] of the campaign, I have only to say that we have beaten the Federal forces in every encounter, and against odds, that from the worst armed, my forces are the best armed in the country.

We reached this point in rags and blanketless. The Army is now well clad and well supplied in other respects.

The entire campaign has been prosecuted without a dollar in the Quarter Master Department, Capt. Harrison not having yet reached this place. But Sir, I can not speak encouragingly for the future. My troops have manifested a dogged irreconcilable detestation of the Country and the People. They have endured much, suffered much and cheerfully, but the prevailing discontent backed up by the distinguished valor displayed on every field, entitle them to marked consideration and indulgence, and, taken in connection with the scant supplies of provisions and the disposition of our own citizens to depreciate our currency may determine me, without waiting for instructions, to move by slow marches down the country both for the purpose of remounting and recruiting our thinned ranks.

Trusting that the management of this more than difficult task imposed upon me by the Government, may prove satisfactory to the President,

I have the honor to be
Very respectfully
Your obdt. Servt.
(Signed)   H. H. Sibley
Brig. Genl.[8]

Genl. S. Cooper

[unrelated note dated January 1874 omitted]

117.

Hd. Qrs., Army of New Mexico
Fort Bliss, May 5th 1862

Genl. S. Cooper
Inspector and Adjutant General
    C.S. Army Richmond Va.
General:

I have the honor herewith to enclose to you the report of Col. James Reily, 4th Regt. Texas Mounted Volunteers, concerning his mission to the government of the Mexican State of Sonora. It is accompanied by documents and correspondence interchanged between him and the Governor of that State.

A perusal of this report and correspondence will I am confident, vindicate the propriety of my action in dispatching Col. Reily upon this service, of which I advised you at the time. That officer appears to have acquitted himself of his duties with much ability and great success, in spite of serious obstacles and difficulties. I commend his suggestions to the attention of the government.

I have the honor, General
to be your obdt. Servt.
(Signed)   H. H. Sibley
Brig. Genl. P.A.C.S.
Comdg. Army of N.M.

118.

Head Quarters, Army of N.M.
Fort Bliss, Texas. May 8, 1862

Colonel.

The Genl. Comdg. directs that you will post one strong company of your Regt. at the Copper Mines for the protection of the parties and persons working the same. Such Company will afford protection to Mr. Lacoste, one of the proprietors of the mines, on his way to them; and the Genl. desires that you will afford him and his operations all the facilities practicable in the way of transportation and otherwise.

These orders are given in consequence of the solicitude expressed by the Confederate government for the successful working of these mines, of the products of which the government stands greatly in need.

Capt. [Thomas J.] Helm's Company, being only for 12 months and that time being nearly expired, is, by the direction of the Genl. Comdg, to proceed to the "Cottonwoods" to be there mustered out of the service, and thus afford its members an opportunity of enlisting for the war.

I am Colonel
your Obt. Servt.

Col. Wm Steele,   (Signed)   A. M. Jackson
7th Regt. T.M. Vols.   A.A.G.

119.

Hd. Qrs., Army of New Mexico
Fort Bliss, Texas. May 8, 1862

Colonel.

Your communication relative to the Recruiting Service and specifying your orders in regard thereto, were received and submitted to the commanding genl., who instructs me to inform you that the orders issued by you, above referred to, are suspended, it being the purpose of the General Comdg. to publish a General Order on the same subject, in due time.

I am, Colonel,
your obdt. Servt.

Col. Jas. Reily,   (Signed)   A. M. Jackson
4th Regt T.M. Vols.   A.A.G.

120.

Hd. Qrs., Army of N.M. A.G.O.
Fort Bliss, Texas. May 8, 1862

Col. W^is L. Robards
Vol. A.D.C. & Chief of Ordnance
Army of New Mexico
Colonel.

I am instructed by the Genl. Comdg. this army, to acknowledge the receipt of your communication of the 5th inst., tendering your resignation as Vol. Aid de Camp and Chief of Ordnance, and to express to you the great regret with which, in justice to you and appreciating the sincerity of your motives, he feels constrained to conform to your request and accept your resignation.

The General at all times and every where will esteem it a duty and a pleasure to bear testimony to your gallant bearing on the field of battle, as well as to the zeal, intelligence, integrity and efficiency, with which you have discharged the duties of the Ordnance Department of this Army. In seeking another field of service, you will bear with you his kindest recollections of your past associations, and his best wishes for your future prosperity and happiness.

I have the honor
Colonel to be
your Obdt. Servt.
(Signed)   A. M. Jackson
A.A.G.

121.

Hd. Qrs., Army of New Mexico, A.G.O.
Ft. Bliss, May 9th 1862

Messrs. Hayward & McGrorty
Mesilla
    Gentlemen:
        The case of Mr. Lemons, held as a prisoner at Mesilla,
by the order of Col. Baylor, and whose property consisting of
certain monies etc., is reported to be in your hands; having been
duly considered by the Genl. Comdg. he instructs me to require at
your hands the restoration of said property, and the release of the
Prisoner.

I am Gentlemen
Your Obdt. Servt.
(Signed)   Jos. E. Dwyer
A.D.C.

122.

Hd. Qrs. Army of New Mex.
Fort Bliss, Texas. May 11, 1862

Colonel
    Yours of the 9th instant has been received and submitted to the
Genl. Comdg. who instructs me to reply to the various matters
contained in it.
    1. The General had understood that Col. Steele had made
sufficient arrangements for the immediate necessities of the troops
in point of transportation by the purchase or employment of two
trains, Barnes & another, and therefore had not imagined that your
command was so destitute in this respect as it is. The difficulties of
procuring transportation here are insurmountable, no doubt for
the same reasons which make it unobtainable in Mesilla. There is a
considerable amount of transportation on the road here brought by
Capt. Harrison & the troops accompanying him. It will arrive in a
few days.

As soon as it does, and it is possible for the Quarter Master to ascertain the amount of transportation belonging to the army, an equitable division of it will be made among the several Corps. All that possibly can be obtained will be, though, as I have said, the prospect here is as unpromising as possible. In the mean time the Genl. knows you will do the best possible under such embarrassments. Of course you will not hesitate to procure such as you may be able to procure.

2. In regard to Bread Stuffs, Orders have been given to Major Brownrigg to supply your wants without delay. Concerning the mill, Maj. Brownrigg has a standing contract with Bull for all the flour it can make. The Genl. is of the opinion that taking the mill out of Bull's ~~hands~~ management may prove an embarrassment to obtaining as full a supply as might be got under the contract. Unless Mr. Bull, therefore, refuses to proceed with his contract, the General thinks it advisable to restore the mill to him, taking proper precautions to insure that the grain on hand be not diverted to other uses than those of the army. Maj. Brownrigg is ready to adjust and settle Mr. Bull's accounts for past supplies. In no event, I am instructed to say, can your troops be straightened [straitened] for Bread Stuffs—there is a sufficiency here as I am informed for all probable wants.

3. Orders have already been issued to the Ordnance Officer to proceed to the Encampment of Baylor's Command, where they shall be paid off, and to collect from it the public arms to which you refer, for the purpose of distributing them among this army.

4. Concerning public animals in private hands, the most stringent orders have already been issued, as I supposed you were aware, for the Quarter Master to reclaim and take them. You will consider yourself fully empowered to enforce these orders within the scope of your means and through the instrumentality of your Quarter Master or any other officer or agent you may designate.

The General instructs me to assure you that every effort ~~will~~ is being made to supply the various wants of the troops which it is possible in this sparse region to make, and he relies greatly on your

earnest & hearty cooperation in these efforts. He desires that you
will not hesitate to ~~act~~ exercise your own judgment and discretion,
in making such arrangements as you may be able to effect, towards
this end.

Having covered all the points in your communication

I am Colonel, your Obdt. Servt.
(Signed)   A. M. Jackson
A.A.G.

P.S. It is important that proper precautions be taken to prevent the
consumption of grain by animals, as all bread stuffs in the valley
will be necessary for the troops.

The General contemplates a herding camp at or near San
Augustine Springs, where grass, water, wood, shade &c. are said to
be fine. He will determine positively tomorrow.

(Signed)   A. M. J.
A.A.G.

Col. Thos. Green
5th Regt. T.M.V.
Las Cruces, Arizona

123.

Head Quarters, Army of N.M.
Fort Bliss, Texas, May 14, 1862

Colonel:

Your communication of yesterday was submitted to the Genl. commanding, and I am instructed to reply.

1st. That in the present exigencies of the service, he does not feel justified in granting the leave of absence requested by you, unless the "circumstances" referred to by you are of such a character as to render such leave an act of justice to you. Without more definite information in regard thereto upon your part, he cannot positively determine, but would be very reluctant to refuse your request if persisted in by you and he should feel authorized to accede to it.

2. Lieut. E. R. Lane was allowed leave of absence and when Col. Scurry's Regiment shall be organized he will be permanently transferred to it. Until then he will of course be borne upon the Rolls of his Company as Lieutenant, whether acceptable therein or no.

3. I enclose the appointment of Lieut. Jno. Reily, as commissary, ranking as Captain of your Regiment.

4. Arrangements will be made for the enrollment provided for by the Conscription Act in due time by the appointment of Special Functionaries for the purpose.

I am, Colonel, &c.

Col. Reily   (Signed)   A. M. Jackson
4th Regt. T.M. Vols.   A.A.G.

124.

Hd. Qrs. Army of New Mexico A.G.O.
Ft. Bliss, Texas, May 15, 1862

Colonel:

In reply to yours of this date regarding Capt. McClau's parole, I have to say that the manner in which you administered it, i.e., upon his honor as an officer, is that in vogue among civilized nations, and is certainly binding on him.

It is presumed that the oaths exacted of an officer, were imposed under misapprehension by ignorant or malignant officials, and are exceptions to the general practice of the Federals.

Therefore the General is of the opinion that we should not adopt these cases as precedents to be followed.

I am Colonel,
Yr. Obt. Servt.
(Signed)   A. M. Jackson
Asst. Adjt. Genl.
Army of New Mexico

Col. Reily
4th Regt. T.M. Vols.

125.

Head Quarters, Army of N.M.
Ft. Bliss, Texas, May 17, 1862

Genl. S. Cooper
Adjt. & Insp. Genl.
Army of Confederate States,
    Richmond, Va.
General:

In consequence of the communications of this Army having been cut off during the recent campaign made by it in New Mexico, it has not been practicable to transmit to your office copies of the orders at the proper stipulated periods.

I have now the honor of forwarding herewith transcripts of the General Orders of the Hd Qrs, No 10 to 22 inclusive, and of Special Orders No. 23 to 66 inclusive bringing the same down to the first day of the present month.

I have the honor to be your
Obt. Servt.
A. M. Jackson, AAG

126.

Hd Qrs Army of New Mexico
Fort Bliss, Texas May 17, 1862

To His Excellency
    Don Luis Terrazas
        Governor of the State
            Of Chihuahua

I have the honor to acknowledge the receipt of your communication of date of the [17th] day of [March] 1862, informing me of a certain incursion made upon the territory of your state by a force under Col. John R. Baylor of the Confederate Army and complaining of injuries or depredations upon your citizens perpetuated thereby.

I assure you, Sir, that I receive this information with great regret. The policy of the Confederate States which I have been anxious to effectuate is to cherish the most amicable relations with all foreign nations and more particularly with the Mexican States whose geographical position must always render their good will desirable to the Confederacy.

About two months since Col. John R. Baylor resigned his commission and left the army and country to go, as I am informed to the seat of the Confederate Government at Richmond, Va. Had I received your complaint before he left, it would have promptly discharged to have held him answerable for the matter of which you inform me. In as much as he has resigned and departed beyond the lines of this Army, you will at once perceive that I have it no longer within my immediate power to institute measures upon the subject.

Under these circumstances, I shall this day forward your communication to the proper Department of the Confederate Government at Richmond, Va. and I doubt not it will meet prompt action and such as will prove satisfactory to you.

I shall request my Government to inform you in relation thereto, and shall not fail upon this or any future occasion to give evidence by my action of the desire of my government and of myself to do prompt justice to your government and people and to cultivate the most friendly relations with them.

I have the honor, Sir, to be

your Obdt. Servt.

(Signed)   H. H. Sibley

Brig Genl

Commanding

127.

Head Quarters, Army of New Mexico, A.G.O.
Fort Bliss, May 23, 1862

Sir:

I am today in receipt of your two communications to me of date April 25th and 26th, accompanied by an extract from your general order No. 38, and a list of prisoners of war in our power or on parole for whom you propose to exchange.

Your proposal would be unequivocally accepted but that it appears proper I should communicate to you that an exchange for these same prisoners was substantially, though in a very objectionable form, effected with Col. G. H. Paul of your forces, early in April last, of which fact, I infer you have not been informed.

A proposition for this exchange was, in the first instance, as I was apprized, transmitted through Capt. Lewis and Capt. Ford of your forces, to Lt. Col. Scurry of this Army then commanding at Santa Fe.

No determinate arrangement having been effected at the interview between those officers, I despatched my Asst. Adjt. Genl. Major A. M. Jackson and my Aid de Camp, Capt. J. E. Dwyer under a Flag of Truce to the Commanding Officer of your forces in that section of the Territory, at that time Col. Paul. An interview between the bearers of the flag and Col. Paul was had at San José on the 9th of April, and the propositions made to Col. Paul were taken by him under consideration with the promise of an answer within two hours.

The "Answer" subsequently but on the same day furnished by Col. Paul was in the shape of a "Special Order" with an "additional" order superadded, from which I extract and herewith transmit to you so much as pertains to the exchanges. This mode of effecting exchanges being deemed offensive in form, and unprecedented in practice, another interview was demanded with Col. Paul at his camp a few miles from San José, by the officers bearing the flag. The interview however was declined.

Under these circumstances I should not have regarded Col. Paul's *ex parte* mode of proceedings as entitled to any notice. But considering it equivalent to putting the prisoners whom we had taken and paroled, back upon duty in your ranks, and being averse to regarding them while acting under the orders of their commanding officer as violating their paroles and incurring severe penalties, I acquiesced in the arrangement set forth in the "Special Order" as a substantial exchange, and have ever since so regarded it.

You will perceive that this arrangement covers all the prisoners of war taken by us who are included in the list forwarded by you.

There is another, however, and a larger body of prisoners taken and paroled by us whose cases have not been disposed of. I refer to the command of Col. Nicholas Pino, of New Mexican troops, who were captured, in a body at Socorro by Lt. Col. H. C. McNeill and his command a few days after the battle of Valverde. Col. Paul at the interview before mentioned declined to exchange for these prisoners, though I am at a loss to conceive upon what principle. It matters not whether they were militia, Volunteers or Regulars. I presume it can not be denied that they constituted a portion of your forces, served under your command against the Confederate States forces, and were in every sense in the service of the United States.

These prisoners were over two hundred in number, and under the command of Col. N. Pino and Major Jesus Maria Baca y Salazar, officers who were also taken prisoner and paroled. This number exceeds that of the Confederates in your hands or under your parole.

You are under a misapprehension in regard to the point of view in which surgeons have been and are regarded by the Armies of the Confederate States and this Army in particular.

Dr. Gray was arrested for reasons wholly independent of his profession or his connection with the U.S. Army. For Col. Baylor's conduct I do not hold myself responsible nor, if he treated surgeons as combatants, do I believe it at all conformable to the practice of the government he serves. A surgeon of your Colorado troops was taken by us at Peralta and released without parole or exchange, and his passport beyond our lines will show you that officers of his profession were not regarded as proper subjects for capture. I therefore consider and give you this as assurance that your surgeons Gray, McKee and Alden are released from parole.

I avail myself of the opportunity of forwarding to you a letter received from the father of the late Capt. McRae who was killed at Valverde. I feel it necessary to command his requests to your favorable consideration.

In conclusion, I take pleasure in acknowledging the humanity and kindness with which, so far, as I am informed, my sick and wounded have been treated while within your power.

I am most Respectfully
Your Most Obdt. Servt.
(Signed)   H. H. Sibley
Brig. Gen, Commanding
Army of New Mexico

Col. E. R. S. Canby
Comdg U.S. forces in
New Mexico, Santa Fe

128.

Hd Qrs, Army of New Mexico, AAG
Fort Bliss, Texas, May 24, 1862

Colonel:

The General Comdg directs that you will select and order down to this post a commissioned officer of your Regiment to relieve Lieut. H. G. Carter (4th Regt) as quarter master and commissary at this post. He desires that this may be done with as little delay as practicable for reasons that the necessary inventories of property will require some time.

I am further directed to state to you that in the General's opinion the parole imposed upon Dr. H. Hunter of Capt. Gardner's Company in no degree disqualifies him from acting in the capacity of a Surgeon. (If my own opinion were worth stating I would give it clearly to the same effect.) Therefore if agreeable to yourself and Dr. Hunter, it is desired that he comes down here to be put upon duty (I suppose with a regular appointment) in the Medical Staff.

I am Colonel
Your Friend & obdt. Servt.
(Signed)   A. M. Jackson
A.A.G.

Col. Wm Steele
Com^{dg} 7th Rgt. T.M. Vols.
Doña Ana, Arizona

129.

Head Quarters, Army of New Mexico, A.G.O.
Fort Bliss, Texas, May 29, 1862.

Colonel:

Capt. Harrison makes an urgent request that a return of the *casualties* among the Officers of the different Regiments of this Army be furnished him, showing the deaths, resignations &c, since the organization of each Regiment. As the information has never been in my office, I am compelled to call upon the Regiments for it. Capt. H. needs it as evidence upon which he can pay the Commissioned Officers upon their pay accounts. The return should show the date at which the Officer, if one of the original ones, was mustered in; if he has been appointed or elected since, it should show the date at which he was elected or appointed.

He also calls for returns of the strength, present and absent, on 31st of this month, of each Regiment. This is necessary to him as a basis for his estimates for funds required for the future pay of the troops, and the other necessities of his Department.

I have been able to obtain a very few monthly Post Returns, which your Companies can use in making out this return, and which I send herewith. I also send a Department return, which your Adjutant can use as a Regimental Return, upon which to consolidate those of the Companies. It is requested by Capt. H. that these Returns be sent down as early as practicable in as much as he needs them at once.

I am Colonel
Very respectfully, your Friend

(Signed)   A. M. Jackson

Asst. Adjt. Genl.

Col. Thos. Green
5th Regt. T.M.V.

130.

Head Quarters, Army of New Mexico, A.G.O.
Fort Bliss, May 29th 1862

Colonel:

I enclose you the following papers pertaining to your
Regiment:

1. Certificate of discharge for Jas. S. Phillips of Capt. Cleaver's
Company. When this was received and acted on Jany. 28, our
information was that the Companies of Capt. Cleaver and Kirksey
were on their route to this army. Consequently the certificate was
retained.

2. Dr. Cupples' certificate for the discharge of John W. Watts,
private, Company "F" of your Regiment. There being no
certificate of the Officer in command of the Company, no
discharge could be ordered.

3. Five certificates for discharge from different companies of your
Regiment, sent back here from Richmond for corrections, which I
mentioned in a former communication relative to this and others.
These have already received your endorsement of the time of
discharge, but your signature does not appear to the endorsements.
In order that these papers may not re-visit us again from
Richmond, please attach your signature and mail them to A. Genl.
at Richmond.

In the next place, Capt. Harrison is urgent for a List of the
Casualties among Officers of the several Regiments since their
organization, showing dates &c. In order that he may have proper
evidence in his office upon which to pay them as they apply.

Please have Lieut. Howard to make a consolidated return of
the casualties from your several Companies and forward it to
Capt. H. as early as practicable.

And lastly, to furnish Capt. Harrison with a basis for his estimates, please have a report of the full strength of your command, present and absent, as of May 31st, made to this office.

I am Colonel,
Very respectfully
Your obt. Servt.

Col. Steele   (Signed)   A. M. Jackson
7th Regt. T.M.V.   A.A.G.

P.S. I also enclose, with proper order endorsed, the certificate for the discharge of Wm S. Phillips of Capt. Cleaver's Company.

Under separate cover I send some Post Returns (blanks) which your Companies can use in making returns above called for. Also a blank Department Return, which can be adapted to the Regimental Return. My box of blanks was left in Albuquerque by the neglect of my clerk, which fact I never ascertained until we got back to Las Cruces.

Yours respectfully
(Signed)   A. M. J.

131.

Head Quarters, Army of New Mexico, A.G.O.
Fort Bliss, Texas, May 29th 1862.

Capt. J. B. McCown
Provost Marshal
    Mesilla Aza.
Captain:

Your communication of the 21st inst., with the accompanying papers relative to the settlement you were directed to make with the Receiver of Sequestrated property at Mesilla, was received several days since and submitted to the General Commanding, who immediately instructed me to express to you his views relative to the several points so clearly submitted by you for his determination. In accordance with his direction, I should have done so before this date, but for an indisposition which has for several days disabled me from attention to business.

It is not considered at all necessary to review much of what has been submitted by Mr. S. Hare to you and Capt. Loebnitz upon the subject in question. One or two remarks dispose of the whole of it.

1st. Although Section 21 of the Sequestration Act *does* provide that "Treasury notes of this Confederacy" shall be received for Sequestrated effects, yet neither it nor any other section of that or any other act makes any such provision in regard to Quarter Masters receipts, or vouchers. These latter are in no sense "~~Quarter~~ Government paper" as Mr. Hare appears to imagine. They are subject at any time to rejection for frauds, or mistake or many other reasons appearing to the disbursing Officer to whom they are presented.

In short, they were not legally receivable, and Judge Hare nor no other power short of the law making power or a military authority administering martial law, could make them receivable. Judge Hare's order to the Receiver to the contrary was clearly void and carried with it no ~~effect~~ authority whatever, because in violation of the distinct law.

The consequence is unavoidable that the Receiver and his Securities are legally liable for the proceeds of the property thus illegally disposed of, and liable in specie or Treasury notes at the option of the Government.

These views are only expressed to dispose of the attempted defense set up for the gross illegality of the Sequestration proceedings in Arizona. But it having been the object of the General Comdg., to render available for the indispensable and pressing wants of the sick and wounded of this Army, the *species funds* which *should* now have represented in the Receiver's hands the property sold by him and that object necessarily failing (if the facts stated be true) for the conclusive reason that the Officers charged with the execution of the law have not the funds, which the law requires they should have, the General Comdg. can have no further purpose to effect in connection with this matter except to protect the Government from further loss from the same source.

It is, therefore, the General's purpose to refer to Col. Wm Steele, Military and Civil Governor of Arizona, the investigations, through Commissions, of the truth of the matters alleged by these parties, and the adoption and execution of measures for the protection of the Government against further loss.

In the meantime the only further action expected from you is to require from Judge Hare a list specifying and describing the Quarter Masters Receipts or Vouchers, which he claims to hold as proceeds of sequestrated property. He having ceased to be judge and having become attorney for claimants against the funds, there is no longer that official responsibility upon him which is contemplated by the loss, but in its place there is an intrust inconsistent with the character of a depository of public moneys. Therefore upon receiving the list of vouchers and receipts you will place in the hands of the Quarter Master at Mesilla a copy of it, together with the enclosed order for stoppage of payment of such vouchers &c. until further orders from proper authority. A copy of the list should also be sent to these Head Quarters.

I need scarcely add that the claims of the interveners nor for the alleged losses are not to be recognized by you in any manner.

Should any new circumstances have come to your knowledge imparting that the Receiver actually obtained specie in whole or in part for the property sold, you are requested to report them, as such facts might materially affect further proceedings in regard to the matter.

I am Captain
Very respectfully
your obdt. Servt.
(Signed)   A. M. Jackson
Asst. Adj. Genl.

132.

Head Quarters, Army of New Mexico, A.G.O.
Fort Bliss, Texas, May 31, 1862.

General S. Cooper,
Adjt. & Insp. General.
    Richmond, Va.
General:

I have the honor herewith to transmit copies of the General and Special Orders issued from the Head Quarters of this Army during the month of May, 1862.

                    I have the honor, General
                    to be your obt. Servt.
          (Signed) A. M. Jackson
                    Asst. Adjt. Genl.
                    Army of New Mexico

133.

Head Quarters, Army of New Mexico A.G.O.
Fort Bliss, Texas, June 1st 1862

Capt. J. B. McCown
    Provost Marshal
    Mesilla, Arizona.
Captain:

Your Guard arrived here this morning bringing with them Mr. Joe Bowers, charged with murder, and the proceedings of the inquest &c.

The General instructs me to send back the prisoner to be kept in your custody until a court or commission can be organized by Col. Steele, Military and Civil Governor, for the disposition of the case.

It is impossible to dispose of the case here for the reasons that the majority of the witnesses are not here and could not be got under several days. Meanwhile, the troops here will have taken up the line of march, which can not be delayed to try this case. The proper depositions would not be admitted.

Col. Steele will be advised in relation to the case from these Head Quarters.

I am Captain
Very respectfully
(Signed)   A. M. Jackson

Inquiry papers &c are returned herewith.   A.A.G.

134.

Head Quarters, Army of New Mexico, A.G.O.
Fort Bliss, Texas, June 1st 1862.

Colonel:

A prisoner (Joe Bowers) of Capt. Helm's Company was brought down here this morning from Mesilla, for trial.

A trial at this place and time is impracticable for the reasons that the majority of the witnesses are not here, and the delay occasioned in bringing them here would postpone the time of trial beyond the time fixed for the march of the troops now here. Consequently the prisoner has been sent back to Mesilla, to be there detailed by the Provost Marshal until by your Order as Civil and Military Governor a Court or Commission shall be organized for the disposition of the case.

The simple object of this communication was to apprize you of this position of the case.

I am Colonel
Very respectfully

Col. Wm Steele,   (Signed)   A. M. Jackson

Civil & Military Govr   A.A.G.

   Arizona

135.

Head Quarters, Army of New Mexico, A.G.O.
Fort Bliss, Texas, June 1st 1862.

Colonel:

On the 12th of the present month, Capt. McCown, Provost Marshal at Mesilla was ordered from these Head Quarters to examine the books, accounts &c. of the Receiver of Sequestrated property for Arizona, and upon such examination to require the payment in specie of such proceeds as should be found in his hands, which were intended to be disbursed for the benefit of the sick and wounded of this Army.

The papers which I now enclose you, by the General's Orders, pertain to the proceedings under this order. They are, 1st, Capt. McCown's communication to these Head Quarters. 2nd, the communication of S. Hare, late Judge, to Capt. McCown. 3rd, the communication of same to Captain Loebnitz, A.Q.M., and 4th, the communication (a copy) from this Office to Capt. McCown.

From this latter document, you will observe that the matter is referred to you for such proceedings as you shall institute in regard thereto. This has been done because in the condition of all the troops of this Army, except those which are to remain under your Command, it was impracticable to organize the proper Commission from these Head Quarters, for the disposition of the case, and further because it appears more appropriate to you as Civil and Military Governor of Arizona.

You will observe also, that certain precautionary measures have been directed in the communication from this office to Capt. McCown. These of course are subject to such change or modification as you may direct.

I am Colonel
Very respectfully
(Signed)   A. M. Jackson
A.A.G.

Col. Wm Steele

136.

Head Quarters, Army of New Mexico
Fort Bliss, Texas, June 2nd 1862.

Sir:

Your letter of the 27th ultimo, making certain enquiries in reference to your duties as commissary of subsistence, has been duly received. In regard to the Mexican affairs, I would advise that their act^s [accounts] be transferred to Col. Steele's Commissary. As to the unpaid accounts of diseased [deceased] officers, I would make an abstract of them with an explanatory letter, describing the lack of money to make cash payments. Send direct to the Commissary General in Richmond, include [Marion B.] Wyatt's Act. in this abstract.

Very respectfully yours
(Signed)   H. H. Sibley

Capt. Beck

137.

Head Quarters, Army of New Mexico
Fort Bliss, Texas, June 2nd, 1862.

General S. Cooper
Adjutant and Inspector General,
        Richmond, Va.

General:

On the 4th ult. I had the honor of addressing you a full and detailed report of the operations of this Army in a recent campaign in New Mexico. In the same communication I also explained the reason why, notwithstanding the signal, repeated and uniform successes of my forces, I was absolutely necessitated to evacuate that Territory and fall back upon Arizona. That reason was the dearth of supplies and the impossibility of obtaining them in quantities at all adequate to the maintenance of this Army.

When that retrograde movement was adopted, it was confidently believed that the resources of Arizona would suffice for my force until supplies could be drawn from the settled portion of Texas; and even up to the date of the communication above referred to I entertained a similar hope.

It becomes now my duty, however to report that the reliance thus placed in Arizona and this remote corner of Texas, has proved to have been misplaced. Although every devisable means have been adopted it has become manifest that, with the exception of the single article of flour, no more supplies are obtainable in this country. Supplies to a considerable amount might indeed be drawn from Chihuahua and Sonora, had we any funds, which would be accepted there in exchange. But no other funds are available there except Specie or English Exchange. Myself and my Chief Quarter Master both made every possible effort to obtain such funds, but without avail.

The proper Department at Richmond, though repeatedly appealed to, failed to supply them, and negotiations for them with Government paper are impossible anywhere within my reach.

My troops have been already reduced for weeks to rations of flour and beef alone, and of the latter there is not on hand a supply equal to their subsistence for ninety days.

Thus circumstanced, no alternative has remained but to order the greater portion of my forces to take up the line of march for the settled portion of this state, where supplies can be obtained. Accordingly the battalion of the 2nd Regt. Texas Mtd Rifles (heretofore in service here under Lt. Col. Baylor) has already been put en route. The 4th and 5th Regiments, Texas Mtd Vols., and the battalion of the 7th Regiment, T.M.V. which with the other Corps made the campaign of New Mexico, and the Battery of Field Artillery taken at Valverde (which I have caused to be ~~named~~ manned and organized) will follow at the earliest practicable periods.

For the defense of Arizona, I leave Col. William Steele, 7th Regt. T.M.V., with a command consisting of 5 Companies of his Regiment, with four Companies of Arizona mounted troops, and Teel's Battery of field Artillery. With my present information of the reduced and disorganized condition of the enemy in New Mexico, I regard this force as adequate to the defense of Arizona. It is certainly as much as can be subsisted even for a period long enough to admit of supplies being sent forward from Texas.

Upon the arrival of the troops in San Antonio, should I receive no instructions to the contrary, it is my purpose to permit the Companies to return to their respective localities, for the purpose of enabling them to obtain horses, clothing and necessaries without which they cannot be restored to a condition of efficiency.

I have the honor, General
To be your obt. Servt.
(Signed)   H. H. Sibley
Brig. Genl.
Commanding

138.

Hᵈ Qrs., Army of New Mexico, A.G.O.
Fort Bliss, Texas, June 4, 1862.

Colonel:

Your communication of 2ⁿᵈ inst., accompanied by the charges and other documents referred to therein, was received this morning and at once submitted to the General Comdg. In accordance with his instructions I enclose you an Order for a General Court Martial to assemble this day [next] week for the disposition of the cases referred to and all others which may be brought before it.

In reference to a Quarter Master for your Regiment, the General directs me to say that previous to your recommendation of Mr. DeWitt, he had appointed Mr. J. F. Battaile a Captain in the Quarter Master's Dept. and that he has been assigned for duty with your Regiment. The General commends him to your confidence as a man of integrity, industry and efficiency and thinks he will approve [*sic*] himself satisfactory to you in every respect.

I am further directed by the General to suggest that with the object of keeping a proper observation upon the movements of the enemy reported by Captain S. Hunter to be in some force in Western Arizona, he thinks it would be advisable for you to throw out Lt. Col. [Philemon T.] Herbert with an adequate force in that direction. The General, however, in leaving you in command of the C.S. Forces in this Region has no intention of embarrassing you with instructions in regard to your movements or the disposition of your troops, which he is well content to leave to your discretion.

Capt. Harrison, A.Q.M., and Major R. T. Brownrigg, A.C.S., are instructed to turn over for the use of your Command, all the funds in their hands not absolutely necessary to their own immediate expenditure.

I beg to call your attention and ask your early action on the subject matter of my communication to you of May 24th, requesting that you would detail and send down a Commissioned Officer to relieve the Actg. A.Q.M. & A.C.S. of this Post.

I am Colonel

with high respect

Your obt. Servt.

Col. Wm Steele   (Signed)   A. M. Jackson

Comdg 7th Regt. Texas Mtd Vols.   A.A.G.

139.

Head Quarters, Army of New Mexico
Fort Bliss, Texas. June 4, 1862.

General:

I have the honor to report that the following resignations have been tendered, and subject to the approval of his Excellency the President, have been accepted by me.

For sake of greater convenience I have caused them to be put in tabular form, showing the date at which the provisional acceptances were made. In former communications I have briefly explained the necessity, which, however, is sufficiently obvious, for such acceptance in order to maintain the organization of a Force so far removed from the seat of Government. No resignations have been thus acted on except with reference alone to the interest of the service of this Army.

List

Names	Regiment	Company	Date of Acceptance
1st Lieut. W. B. Key	7th T.M. Vols.	"I"	Feby. 18, 1862
Capt. D. A. Nunn	4th " " "	"	" 27, "
" I. C. Stafford	2nd " " Rifles	"E"	" " "
" G. W. Campbell	5th " " Vols	"F"	March 8, "
Asst. Surg. J. F. Matchcett	4th " " "		" 11, "
Chaplain R. W. Peirce	5th " " "		" " "
Asst. Surg. I. W. Cunningham	7th " " "		" " "

Names	Regiment	Company	Date of Acceptance
Capt. J. M. Noble, A.C.S.	4th " " "		" 12, "
1st Lieut. W. A. Shannon	5th " " "	"C"	" 13, "
2nd " F. M. Brown	4th " " "	"F"	" 16, "
1st " W. G. Wilkins	5th " " "	"E"	" 20, "
Capt. M. B. Wyatt, A.Q.M.	5th " " "	"	" 21, "
1st Lieut. J. G. Marshall	5th " " "	"D"	May 16, "
" A. L. Hudiburgh	7th " " "	"	April 20, "
" G. W. Eaton	7th " " "	"	" " "
Capt. A. J. Scarborough	4th " " "	"B"	May 16, "
1st Lieut. J. B. Holland	4th " " "	"	" 17, "
2nd " R. J. Robinson	5th " " "	"I"	" 20, "
2nd " B. W. Loveland	2nd " " Rifles "E"		" 26, "

I also enclose for your information and any official action deemed expedient, an official copy of a letter of resignation received by me from Lieut. Col. Jno. R. Baylor (provisionally appointed Colonel by me as you were advised on the 16 of December last), 2nd R[g]t. T.M.R. I am at a loss to know to what officer allusion is made in the second paragraph of this letter—certainly not at the date of the letter or previous, with any justice to me.

Many of these resignations would have been reported earlier but for the want of communication from New Mexico.

In a separate communication, I advise you of the various provisional appointments made by me during the active operations in New Mexico and since; all of which I respectfully ask the confirmation of his Excellency the President.

I am Sir very Respectfully
Your Obt. Servt.

To   (Signed) H. H. Sibley
Genl. S. Cooper,   Brig. Genl.
Adjt. & Insp. Genl. C.S.A.   Commanding
  Richmond Va.

140.

Head Quarters, Army of New Mexico
Fort Bliss, Texas, June 4, 1862.

General S. Cooper
Adjt. & Insp. General
    C.S. Army
General:

I have the honor to report the following provisional appointments made by me during and since the recent active operations of this Army in New Mexico, confirmations of which I ask at the hands of his Excellency, the President, and that commissions issue to take effect at the dates designated.

Some of them may have already been reported by Capt. T. P. Ochiltree, who was so directed on leaving Albuquerque, as bearer of dispatches. For fear of omission however, the list is here made complete to date.

On the tabulated list below, the numbers of the Special Orders making these appointments are shown, by reference to the copies of which, forwarded to your Office, the reasons for the promotions will appear.

Names	No. of Order	To what Promoted	Date of Promotion
1st Lieut. T. P. Ochiltree	37.	Captain, Adjutant Genls. Dept.	Feby. 21, 1862
Capt. Chas. L. Pyron	38.	Major, Col. J. R. Baylor's New Regiment	” ” ”
Capt. John S. Shropshire	39.	Major, 5th T.M.V. vice Lockridge, killed	” ” ”
Joseph E. Dwyer (Vol. A.D.C.)	42.	Aid de Camp, rank 1st Lieut. v. Ochiltree, promoted.	” ” ”
1st Lieut. Thos. G. Wright	56.	A.Q.M. 5th T.M.V. vice Wyatt, resigned.	March 16, ”

Names	No. of Order	To what Promoted	Date of Promotion
Samuel B. Maney	60.	Asst. Surgeon, 4th T.M.V. vice Wyatt, resigned.	" 22, "
Capt. W. P. Hardeman		Lt. Colonel, 4th T.M.V. v. Scurry, promoted.	" 28, "
Capt. G. J. Hampton		Major, 4th T.M.V. vice Raguet, killed.	" 28, "
Capt. Denman Shannon	111.	Major, 5th T.M.V vice Shropshire, killed.	" 28, "
1st Lieut. & Adjt. J. D. Sayers	66.	Captain of Artillery	April 25, "
Robert [sic Thomas] Dryden	73.	Asst. Surgeon, 7th T.M.V. v. Cunningham, resigned.	May 6, "
J. F. Battaile	82.	A.Q.M. rank Captain.	" 10, "
1st Lieut. John Reily	89.	A.C.S. 4th T.M.V. rank Captain vice Noble, resigned.	" 14, "
Philemon T. Herbert	108.	Lieut. Colonel, Arizona Battalion.	" 24, "
Capt. G. M. Frazer	108.	Major, Arizona Battalion.	" 24, "
T. D. Nettles, Private	61.	To 1st Lieut. Artillery.	June 1, "
William Smith "	[?]	To 2nd "	June 1st "

In consideration of gallant and distinguished conduct, Lieut. Col. Wm R. Scurry (4th Regt. T.M. Vols.) was provisionally appointed Colonel by me, with authority to raise a new Regiment; and for the same reason, Charles L. Pyron (whose name already appears in the foregoing list) was similarly appointed Lieutenant Colonel of such new Regiment. If consistent with the "Conscription Act," of the recent Congress, I ask that these appointments be also confirmed with commissions to run from the 21st of Feby. for the first, and for the last, March 26, 1862, the date of the battle of Glorietta.

By Special Order No. 40, Captain T. T. Teel was appointed a Major of Artillery, a grade which I have since understood, had no existence.

By Special Order No. 41, Capt. Powhatan Jordan, 7th Regt. T.M. Vols., was appointed Major of that Regiment vice Arthur P. Bagby promoted to Lieut. Col., vice J. S. Sutton, killed in action at Valverde. Both of these officers have since informally thrown up their appointments; wherefore I recommend that they be *not* confirmed.

> I have the honor, General
> to be your obt. servt.
> (Signed) H. H. Sibley
> Brig. Genl.
> Commanding

141.

Head Quarters, Sibley's Brigade
San Antonio, Texas, July 22, 1862.

General S. Cooper,
Adjt. & Insp. General,
    Richmond, Va.
General:

I have the honor to report my arrival with my Head Quarters at this place.

On the 4th of May last I forwarded to you by Lieut. Col. Wm R. Scurry, from Fort Bliss, a full report of the operations of my forces in New Mexico and Arizona, up to that date; and in the same communication I informed you of the causes, on account of which—want of supplies and of the means of obtaining them—I should be necessitated to withdraw the troops from that region. In pursuance of the purpose so announced, the 4th Regt. Texas M^{td} Vols. (Col. Reily's) has already arrived at and passed through this place. The 5th Regt. (Col. Green's) will reach here within the next two weeks and be followed very speedily by the first Battalion of the 7th Regt. (Col. Steele's).

By the last mail from Arizona I am in receipt of a communication from Col. Steele, dated at Fort Fillmore, July 4th, by which I am informed that he was making every preparation possible there for the immediate removal of his command, to which cause he is constrained by the impossibility of subsisting them in that section. He had been compelled to resort to coercive measures to obtain animals and other transportation, in the enforcement of which collisions had taken place between parties of the troops and some of the Mexican population. The disturbances, however, were promptly quelled, and our loss in them would prove to be very small, if any.

The Battalion of the 2nd Regt. Texas Mounted Rifles (Col. Ford's) which, under Lieut. Col. Baylor in Arizona and under Major Pyron in New Mexico, served under my command, has arrived here and has been by my orders transferred to this Military Department, to which it regularly pertained.

Having received no orders or instructions from the War Department relative to my movements, I have proceeded to carry out the policy in regard to my troops which I announced to you in my report of the 4th of May, and I now enclose to you a copy of my orders relative thereto. In accordance with my order No. 33, the 4th Regt. (Col. Reily's) has already been, by detached Companies, sent to the localities where it was raised, to be recruited, remounted, and re-equipped. The other corps, as they arrive, will be similarly disposed of. It is the only mode practicable by which those troops can be restored to an efficient condition within a reasonable period.

In consequence of the total suspension of mail facilities to the States east of the Mississippi, I am necessitated to despatch officers as bearers of dispatches, to which capacity I have entrusted this communication to Col. James Reily of the 4th Regt, an officer of whose very important and successful services as Commissioner to the Governments of Chihuahua and Sonora, I have had the honor heretofore of forwarding you full and explicit reports. I ask for Col. Reily every consideration which his rank and valuable services merit.

Any orders designed for me will, I trust, be forwarded as early [as] possible.

I have the honor, General,
to be your Obdt. Servt. &c.
(Signed)   H. H. Sibley,
Brig. Genl. Comdg

142.

Head Quarters, Sibley's Brigade, A.G.O.
San Antonio, Texas, July 22, 1862.

General S. Cooper,
Adjt. & Insp. General C.S.A.
General:

I have the honor to enclose herewith official copies of two communications from Genl. Sibley to you, of date June 4—62; the originals of which were forwarded by mail from Fort Bliss.

The interruption of communications across the Mississippi having rendered it doubtful whether the originals reached you, these copies are forwarded to supply their place, if lost.

I have the honor, General,
to be your obdt. Servt.
A. M. Jackson, A.A.G.

143.

Head Quarters, Sibley's Brigade
San Antonio, Texas, August 1, 1862.

Brig. Genl. P. O. Hébert,
Com^{dg} Trans-Miss^i Dept.
South of Red River
General:

I am in receipt of a communication from Major General J. B. Magruder, through his Asst. Adjt. General, by which I am informed that he has been assigned to the command of the Trans-Mississippi Department, and from which I desire to convey to you the following Extract:

"Genl. Hébert will retain the command of the Dept. of Texas until Genl. Magruder's arrival, but in case of active military operations resulting from an invasion by the enemy, as the ranking officer you will take command of all the troops in the Dept."

In accordance with these instructions and with the principle of military law enunciated by them, it is apparent that a very serious responsibility, involving difficult and complicated duties, may at any time be devolved upon me by the occurrence of the contingency referred to in Genl. Magruder's communication. It appears to me to be equally obvious that in order to be prepared to meet such responsibility and to discharge myself of such duties with efficiency, it is indispensable that I should be possessed of full and accurate information of the military resources of the Department, comprising the number, character, and disposition of its forces, the amount and distribution of its munitions and supplies of every kind, to be depended upon and called in requisition in the event of active military operations.

Whilst I shall be careful to abstain from entrenching in the slightest degree upon your province as Commander of the Department, I feel confident that you will concur in the propriety and the necessity of causing me to be fully informed upon these and all other matters which may appear to you proper to be communicated to me.

In reference to the Brigade under my command which is just returning from distant service in New Mexico, I ask also to be informed whether the supplies and resources of the Department are such that, without prejudice to its service, recourse can be had to them to supply the deficiencies which unavoidably exist to some extent in the Ordnance, Quarter Master's and Commissary's Service of my troops. If such recourse can be had, it will greatly expedite and facilitate my operations in the re-equipment of my forces so as to render them again efficient in the field. More particularly in reference to small arms, of which a slight deficiency may have arisen in the long march from New Mexico, and of which no doubt a large deficiency will exist among the recruits to be assigned to my Regiment, I am apprehensive that much difficulty will be encountered in their procurement, unless the means at your command may enable you to supply them.

Having thus, General, indicated the purposes of this communication, I feel that it is unnecessary to enter into details relative to them, which your own familiarity and experience will enable you readily to supply.

I expect in a few days to proceed to the Eastern portion of this State and perhaps to some portions of the State of Louisiana within your Department, and it would be satisfactory to me, if not inconvenient to you, to be apprized before my departure of your views relative to the matters of which I have written.

> I am, General, Very Respectfully
> Your Obdt. Servt.
> H. H. Sibley
> Brig. Genl. &c.

144.

> Head Quarters, Sibley's Brigade, A.G.O.
> San Antonio, Texas, August 1, 1862.

Major E. F. Gray,
 A.A.A.G.
Sub Military District of Rio Grande
Major:

I am instructed by Brig. Genl. Sibley commanding this Brigade, to communicate to you, for the information of Brig. Genl. [Hamilton P.] Bee Com^{dg} Dist., certain facts in reference to 2nd Lieut. L. [William] Smith of the Valverde Light Battery, who was arrested in this City a few days since upon a charge of desertion from the Artillery Company formerly commanded by Capt. Michling. The case has already been to some extent brought to the knowledge of Gen. Bee.

Lieut. Smith formerly belonged (as a private I believe) to the Artillery Company mentioned. Shortly before the march of the 5th Regt. T. M^{td} Vols. (Col. Green's) belonging to this Brigade for New Mexico, in the fall of last year, Col. Green received from Lieut. Cook, then Com^{dg} the Artillery Company (Capt. Michling being in arrest) a letter or note consenting to or requesting the transfer of Mr. Smith to one of the Companies of his (Col. Green's) Regiment. Mr. Smith did enter the service in one of Col. Green's Companies and was from that [date] put upon detached service with the Artillery Corps of the Regiment, with which he served with entire fidelity and great efficiency throughout the late campaign in New Mexico, acting as Drill-Master. His conduct at Valverde, Glorietta and Peralta was such as to procure him the commendations of his commanders and the applause of his comrades. When the Valverde Light Battery was organized, about two months since, he was elected its Second Lieutenant by the Company—which has thus borne its highest testimony to his fidelity as a soldier and to the value of his services.

It is within the recollection of Gen. Sibley that several soldiers belonging to other Corps applied to him to be transferred to the troops under his command, and the General believes, though he cannot positively state, that Mr. Smith was one of them. The General is convinced from his own impressions, from Col. Green's statements, and from all the circumstances surrounding the case, that there could have been no intentional desertion on the part of Mr. Smith, and that he acted in the belief and probably upon the assurance of others that he had been legally transferred to Col. Green's Regiment.

In this belief and confident that Gen. Bee will sympathize in his solicitude for a gallant man who has rendered very efficient service in three actions, Gen. Sibley respectfully requests that Gen. Bee will make such orders as will not only release Lieut. Smith from his arrest, but also remove forever from his reputation any opprobriums which a charge so disgraceful is calculated to attach to it.

> I am, Major, Very Respectfully,
> Your Obdt. Servt.
> A. M. Jackson
> Asst. Adjt. Genl. Sibley's Brigade

145.

Head Quarters, Sibley's Brigade, A.G.O.
San Antonio, Texas, August 18, 1862.

Lieut. Col. A. P. Bagby,
7th Regt. T.M. Vols.

Lieut. Colonel:

Your letter of resignation of date April 16, 1862, addressed to Adjutant General Cooper, and certain charges forwarded to that officer, have been returned by him to the General commanding this Brigade with the following endorsement.

"Adjt. & Insp. Genl's. Office, Richmond, July 7, 1862.

"Respectfully forwarded to the General commanding Department of New Mexico.

"The resignation of Lt. Col. Bagby will not be accepted, and the Secretary of War directs that a Court of Enquiry be convened in this case, according to paragraph 1, General Orders 38, Current Series, herewith enclosed." "By command of the Secy. of War."

(Signed) "Jno. [John] Withers, Asst. Adjt. Genl."

In accordance with which direction of the Secretary of War, a Court of Enquiry has been ordered by the General Com^{dg} this Brigade, and I herewith enclose to you the order convening it. I also enclose an official copy of the charges, and also of the General Orders of the War Department referred to in the endorsement above set forth.

The General Com^{dg} accordingly directs that you will appear for trial before the Court at the time and place specified in the order.

I am, Lieut. Col.
Your Obdt. Servt.
A. M. Jackson
A.A.G.

You can address me or the Recorder (Lt. Howard) at this place in reference to any witnesses you may desire.

146.

Office of Asst. Adjt. Genl.
Sibley's Brigade, San Antonio, Aug. 27, 1862.

Capt. C. M. Mason,
Asst. Adjt. Genl., Dept. Of Texas
Captain:

I beg leave to transmit for the information of the General Com^{dg} Dept. a communication addressed to me by Maj. R. T. Brownrigg, A.C.S. of this Brigade, and its enclosures—all having reference to the Special Order of the General Com^{dg} Dept. relating to the War Tax funds at Austin.

Should the General Com^{dg} Dept. direct further action in regard to the matter, I respectfully solicit such information in relation thereto as will enable me to respond to Maj. Brownrigg's call for advices upon the subject.

I am, Captain, Very respectfully
Your Obdt. Servt.

A. M. Jackson, A.A.G. S.B.

147.

Office of Asst. Adjt. Genl.
Sibley's Brigade, Oct. 31, 1862

General S. Cooper,
Adjt. & Insp. General,
   Richmond, Va.
General:

After many ineffectual efforts I am at this day enabled to forward a list of paroled men and prisoners still in the hands of the enemy, belonging to the 5th Regt. (Col. Green's) Texas Mtd Vols. I have also the honor to transmit herein the Report of Lt. Col. H. C. McNeill, 5th Texas Mtd Vols. of his capture at Socorro, New Mexico, in February last of Col. Nicholas Pino and his command of New Mexican Militia in the service of the U.S. The written paroles of Col. Pino, Lieut. Col. Jesus Baca y Salazar and Maj. Wesche are also forwarded. By reference to Col. McNeill's Report, it will be seen that he captured, besides these officers, seven Captains and 237 rank and file—of whom, however, he took no list in detail.

Subsequent to this capture and about the 8th of April, I was dispatched by Brig. Genl. Sibley with a flag of truce to the Head Qrs. of Col. Paul U.S.A. at a distance of about 50 miles from Santa Fe for the purpose of arranging an exchange of prisoners. Col. Paul would not recognize any obligation to exchange for these prisoners captured by Lt. Col. McNeill, alleging as a reason that they were Territorial Militia. He did not, however, deny that they were in the service of the U.S.

Genl. Canby U.S.A. Comdg in New Mexico, was afterwards informed by Genl. Sibley of these captives and a demand made for exchanges for them—but no reply was ever received.

Notwithstanding repeated calls, I am not yet in receipt of returns of paroled men and prisoners belonging to the 4th and 7th Regiments Texas Mtd Vols., pertaining to this Brigade.

I have the honor, General
to be your obdt. Servt.
A. M. Jackson,
A.A.G.

N O T E S

INTRODUCTION

1. T. T. Teel, "Sibley's New Mexico Campaign: Its Objects and the Causes of Its Failure," *Battles and Leaders of the Civil War* (New York: Castle Books, 1956), 2:700.

2. Ibid.

3. Donald S. Frazier, *Blood and Treasure: Confederate Empire in the Southwest* (College Station: Texas A&M University Press, 1995), 101–103; Martin Hardwick Hall, "Colonel James Reily's Diplomatic Mission to Chihuahua and Sonora," *New Mexico Historical Review* 31 (July 1956): 232–245. Also, L. Boyd Finch, *Confederate Pathway to the Pacific: Major Sherod Hunter and Arizona Territory, C.S.A.* (Tucson: Arizona Historical Society, 1996).

4. S. Cooper to H. H. Sibley, July 8, 1861, *The War of the Rebellion: A Compilation of the Official Records of the Union and Confederate Armies* (Washington, D.C.: U.S. Government Printing Office, 1889), Ser. 1, Vol. 4:93. These records will hereafter be referred to as *O.R.*

5. George Wythe Baylor, *Into the Far, Wild Country: True Tales of the Old Southwest*, ed. Jerry Thompson (El Paso: Texas Western Press, 1996), 181–207.

6. *Dallas Herald*, August 21, 1861. Also, *Texas State Gazette,* August 10, 1861; Jerry D. Thompson, *Colonel John Robert Baylor: Texas Indian Fighter and Confederate Soldier* (Hillsboro, Texas: Hill College Press, 1971), 24–48.

7. Jerry Thompson, *Confederate General of the West: Henry Hopkins Sibley* (College Station: Texas A&M University Press, 1996), and Max Heyman, *Prudent General: A Biography of Major-General E.R.S.*

Canby, 1817–1873: His Military Service in the Indian Campaigns, in the Mexican War, in California, New Mexico, Utah, and Oregon; in the Civil War in the Trans-Mississippi West and as Military Governor in the Post-War South (Glendale, California: Arthur H. Clark Co., 1959).

8. John Taylor, *Bloody Valverde: A Civil War Battle on the Rio Grande, February 21, 1861* (Albuquerque: University of New Mexico Press, 1995); Don E. Alberts, *The Battle of Glorieta: Union Victory in the West* (College Station: Texas A&M University Press, 1998); Thomas S. Edrington and John Taylor, *Battle of Glorieta Pass: A Gettysburg in the West, March 26–28, 1862* (Albuquerque: University of New Mexico Press, 1998).

9. John P. Wilson, "Whiskey at Fort Fillmore: A Story of the Civil War," *New Mexico Historical Review* 68 (April 1993): 109–132, and Francis C. Kajecki, "The Battle of Glorieta: Was the Guide Ortiz or Grzelachowski?" *New Mexico Historical Review* 62 (January 1987): 47–54.

10. Composed of the captured Federal guns from Valverde, the battery had come to symbolize the courage of the men of the Sibley Brigade. Named for the attending physician at his birth and one of five children, Nettles was born near Darlington, South Carolina, February 14, 1838. Nettles died at the age of eighty-five on October 20, 1923, and was buried in the family cemetery on his farm south of Buffalo, Texas. P. D. Browne, "Captain T. D. Nettles and the Valverde Battery," *Texana* 2 (1964): 1–4.

11. Martin Hardwick Hall, *The Confederate Army of New Mexico* (Austin: Presidial Press, 1978), 148, 213, 290.

12. Browne, "Captain T. D. Nettles," 1.

13. *Fairfield Recorder,* July 29, 1898, quoting the *Seguin Anchor.*

14. Henry Putnam Beers, *Guide to the Archives of the Government of the Confederate States of America* (Washington, D.C.: National Archives and Records Service, 1968), 540-541, 714. Colonel Steele's letterbook survives in Record Group 109, Confederate Trans-Mississippi Department, National Archives, Washington, D.C.

15. Beers, *Guide to the Archives of the Confederate States,* 415–418.

16. See Sibley to Cooper, February 22, 1862, *O.R.,* 1, 9:505–506.

17. Sibley to Cooper, March 31, 1862, *O.R.,* 1, 9:540-541; Sibley to H. P. Bee, May 27, 1862, *O.R.,* 1, 9:714.

18. Bob Cunningham, "The Mystery of the Missing Army Train," *Password* 38 (Spring 1993): 29-41. Also, Frazier, *Blood and Treasure,* 143.

19. W. W. Mills, *Forty Years at El Paso, 1858-1898* (El Paso: Carl Hertzog, 1962), 73\-75.

20. Sherod Hunter jacket, National Archives, Record Group 109, Confederate War Department, M-323, Roll 182.

21. Jefferson Davis to H. H. Sibley, June 7, 1862, *O.R.,* 1, 9:717-718.

22. Thompson, *Henry Hopkins Sibley,* 306.

23. Teel, "Sibley's New Mexico Campaign," 2:700.

24. Thompson, *Henry Hopkins Sibley,* 307.

LETTERS

1. See Sibley to Cooper, November 8, 1861, *O.R.,* 1, 4:132.

2. See Sibley to Cooper, November 16, 1861, *O.R.,* 1, 4:141-143 (published with minor editing and different date).

3. See Sibley to [Luis Terrazas], December 27, 1861, *O.R.,* 1, 4:168.

4. See Sibley to James Reily, December 31, 1861, *O.R.,* 1, 4:167-168.

5. See Sibley to Cooper, January 3, 1862, *O.R.,* 1, 4:167.

6. See Sibley to Cooper, January 27, 1862, *O.R.,* 1, 4:169-170 (published with different date).

7. See Sibley to E. R. S. Canby, February 22, 1862, *O.R.,* 1, 9:632 (published with different date).

8. See Sibley to Cooper, May 4, 1862, *O.R.,* 1, 9:506-512 (published with minor editing).

INDEX

A

Albuquerque, N. M., 2, 129; Sibley
    letters from, 129-32; 138, 140
Alden, Charles Henry, 156
Apache Canyon, N. M., 4
Armijo, Manuel, 141
Armijo, Rafael, 141
Austin, Tex., 22

B

Baca y Salazar, Jesús María, 10, 155,
    183
Bagby, Arthur P., 9, 59, 70, 174, 181
Battaile, J. F., 9, 169, 173
Baylor, John Robert, 3, 6-7, 12, 32,
    69, 73, 82, 85, 91-93, 99, 104, 110-
    19, 121-24, 133, 147-48, 152-53,
    168, 171, 175
Beaumont, Henry, 38
Beck, Joseph H., 8, 119, 166
Bee, Hamilton P., 6, 12, 179, 180
Beers, Henry P., 11
Benjamin, Judah P., 5
Bowers, Joe, 8, 163-164
Bracht, Felix, 70

Bronough, John Mitchell, 11, 70
Brown, F. M., 171
Brownrigg, Richard T., 7, 10, 35,
    37, 58, 148, 169, 182
Buffalo, Tex., 4
Bull, Thomas J., 15, 148
Bullard, W. J., 103

C

Campbell, George Washington,
    103, 170
Canby, Edward Richard Sprigg, 3,
    10, 12, 106, 183
Carter, Henry G., 8, 157
Carver, E. P., 103
Cator, Thomas, 137
Chihuahua, Mex., 2, 7, 14, 89-90, 95,
    100, 123, 167, 176
Chilton, Robert Hall, 5, 118
Clark, Edward, 6, 21-23, 30, 32, 36,
    39-40, 43, 48, 59, 77
Cleaver, William H., 9, 159-60
Cook, H. W., 39
Cooper, Samuel, 5, 12; Sibley letters
    to, 24, 32-33, 40, 45, 50, 52, 54,

Cooper, Samuel (continued)
    57, 67-70, 72, 76, 81-82, 84, 89,
    97, 99-100, 116, 119-20, 133, 142,
    152, 163, 167, 172, 175, 177
Coopwood, Bethel, 7, 110, 140
Covey, Edward, 7, 124
Crosby, Josiah F., 9-10, 16, 69, 75
Cubero, N. M., 132, 136
Cunningham, I. W., 71, 170
Cupples, George, 9, 70, 159

D
Davis, Jefferson, 1, 5, 13, 16
DeWitt, B. J., 169
Doherty, John F. F., 57
Doña Ana, N. M., 124, 133, 140
Dryden, Thomas, 173
Durfee, Charles, 24, 32
Dwyer, Joseph E., 7, 96, 126, 147,
    154, 172

E
Eaton, George W., 171
El Paso, Tex., 1, 9-10, 14-16, 61, 73,
    96

F
Ford, James H., 154
Ford, John "RIP" Salmon, 82, 175
Fort Bliss, Tex., 2-3, 9, 61; Sibley
    letters from, 81-109; 133-74; 143,
    175, 177
Fort Craig, N. M., 2, 15, 99, 125-26,
    134-39
Fort Fillmore, N. M., 3, 6, 108, 175
Fort Leavenworth, Kansas, 14

Fort Quitman, Tex., 89
Fort Stanton, N. M., 3, 138
Fort Thorn, N. M., Sibley letters
    from, 110-28; 134
Fort Union, N. M., 1-2, 137-38
Franklin, Tex., See El Paso, Tex.
Frazer, George Milton, 8, 173
Fulcrod, Phillip, 8, 65, 101

G
Galisteo, N. M., 137
Giddings, George H., 10, 39, 74
Glorieta, N. M., Battle of, 4, 8, 10,
    16, 174, 180
Goldsberry, A. P., 97
Gonzales, Tex., 32
Gorgas, Josiah, 5, 74-75
Graffrath, Jacob, 121
Gray, Edward F., 6, 179
Green, Tom, 8, 18, 26, 37-38, 44-45,
    69, 71, 73, 79, 81, 101, 103, 105,
    119, 134-35, 137-40, 149, 158,
    175, 180, 183
Greenwood, Thomas Benton, 71
Guaymas, Mex., 81

H
Haden, Guy, 24
Hampton, George James, 84, 173
Hare, Silas, 161-162, 165
Hardeman, William Polk, 7, 83, 173
Harris, William H., 97
Harrison, William Henry, 7, 10, 35,
    58, 68, 76, 118, 142, 147, 158-60,
    169
Hart, Simeon, 9-10, 16, 69, 114

Hébert, Paul O., 66-67, 173, 177
Helm, Thomas J., 8, 144, 164
Hempstead, Tex., 83
Herbert, Philemon T., 6, 8, 78-79, 169
Hines, W., 103
Holbert, J. S., 103
Holden, Jesse H., 7, 121
Holland, James B., 83, 171
Howard, Thomas C., 9, 55, 57, 159, 181
Hudiburgh, Alfred L., 171
Hunter, Henry Jacob, 157
Hunter, Sherod, 9, 112, 114-17, 124, 169
Hyatt, Marion B., 71

J
Jackson, Alexander Melvorne, 12, 36-38, 41; letters drafted by, 36-183; 154
Johnston, Albert Sidney, 36
Jordan, Powhatan, 9, 137, 174

K
Key, William B., 170
Kirk, William, 14-15, 123-125
Kirksey, William L., 9, 159
Knights of the Golden Circle, 14-15

L
Lacoste, J. B., 85, 144
Lambane, R. B., 41
Lane, Ellsberry R., 150
Lang, Willis L., 8

Lemon, John, 15, 111, 147
Lewis, William H., 154
Lockridge, Samuel, 8, 27, 37-38
Loebnitz, Henry Edmund, 8, 84, 161, 165
Looscan, Michael, 7, 110, 119
Los Lunas, N. M., 138-39
Loveland, Benjamin W., 171
Lubbock, Francis R., 6, 33

M
Macklin, Sacfield, 46, 78
Magoffin, James, 16
Magruder, John B., 6, 177-78
Maney, Samuel B., 173
Manzano, N. M., 131, 138
Marshall, Crittenden, 15
Marshall, Jacob George, 171
Mason, Charles M., 6, 182
Matchcett, Jacob Frederick, 70, 170
McCown, Jerome B., 8, 64, 160, 163, 165
McCulloch, Henry E., 6, 25, 63, 66, 78-79
McKee, James Cooper, 156
McNeill, Henry C., 8, 10, 21-23, 27, 37-38, 47, 103, 129, 155, 183
McPhaill, John R., 70
McRae, Alexander, 156
Mesilla, N. M., 10, 15, 85, 89, 91, 99, 118-19, 123, 147, 162, 164
Mesilla Valley, N. M., 1-3, 5-6, 8, 14, 86
Michling, Captain, 179
Minter, J. F., 118

Monigle, Mr., 10, 95

Montano, Lorenzo, 130

Myers, Abraham C., 5, 118

N

Navajo Expedition, 17

Nettles, Timothy Dargan, 4, 173

Noble, James M., 8, 119, 171

Noble, S. F., 41

Northrop, Lucius B., 5, 58

Nunn, Samuel, 103, 170

O

Ochiltree, Thomas P., 7, 26, 30-31, 34-35, 109, 172

Ogden, M. L., 9, 70

Owen, Clark L., 42

P

Papago Indians, 127

Paul, Gabriel H., 10, 154-55, 183

Pelham, William, 9, 138

Peirce, R.W., 8, 44, 170

Peralta, N. M., 138, 180

Pesqueíra, Ignacio, 86-88

Phillips, James S., 159

Phillips, John G., 9, 111, 137

Phillips, William S., 160

Pierce, R. W., 8, 44, 170

Pima Indians, 127

Pino, Nicolás, 10, 155, 183

Pueblo Indians, 127

Pyron, Charles Lynn, 7, 136-38, 172-73, 175

R

Raguet, Henry, 8, 34, 37-38, 90, 102

Reily, James, 28, 37-38, 47, 53, 60, 62, 69, 73, 79, 81, 84-85, 90, 95, 100, 114, 116, 118, 127, 135, 143-45, 175-76

Reily, John, 8, 134, 150, 173

Ringgold Barracks, Tex., 41

Robards, Willis L., 13, 67, 80, 120, 126, 146

Roberts, Benjamin S., 92

Robinson, R. J., 171

S

San Antonio, Tex., 10, 21; letters sent from, 25-81; 168

Santa Fe, N. M., 2-3, 9, 134, 136-38, 140

Saxton, B. B., 95

Sayers, Joseph D, 4, 8, 43, 45, 51, 173.

Scarborough, Andrew Jackson, 171

Scurry, William Read, 31, 37-38, 85, 128, 131, 135, 137-39, 154, 173, 175

Selden, Henry R., 92

Shaaff, Arthur, 49-50, 53, 56, 67-68

Shannon, Denman William, 8, 44, 128, 173

Shannon, William A., 171

Shropshire, John Samuel, 4, 8, 137, 172

Sibley, Henry Hopkins, 1-4, 10, 12-13, 16-21; letters by, 21-183

Simmons, William, 7, 99

Smith, William, 173, 179-180

Socorro, N. M., 7, 136, 140, 155

Sonora, Mex., 2, 14, 86-90, 96, 100, 167, 176

Southworth, Malek A., 70

Stafford, Isaac C., 7, 122, 170

Steele, William, 9, 11, 51-52, 69, 72-73, 79, 81, 137, 144, 147, 157, 160-164, 166, 168, 170, 175

Stephenson, Hugh, 108

Sumner, Edwin Vose, 40

Sutton, John S., 9, 54, 135, 174

T

Taylor, L. M., 70, 124

Teel, Trevanion T., 7, 17, 113, 134, 168, 174

Terrazas, Luis, 6, 95, 152

Terry, Davis S., 33

Testard, Adolphe, 97

Thompson, Wiley J., 97

Thurmond, Alfred Sturgis, 9, 132

Tucson, Arizona, 115

V

Valverde Battery, 4, 179-180, 186 n10

Valverde, N. M., Battle of, 4, 48, 10, 12, 16, 133-36, 141, 174, 180

Van Dorn, Earl, 6, 21, 23-25, 33, 35-36, 63, 78

W

Walker, Leroy Pope, 5, 22

Waller, Edwin Jr., 7, 82

Watts, John W., 159

Wesche, Charles Emil, 183

Whitner, H. T., 103

Wilkerson, A., 103

Wilkins, William Gaston, 171

Withers, John, 181

Wood, William S., 8, 65, 101, 134

Wright, Thomas G., 172

Wulff, A. F., 83

Wyatt, Marion B., 8, 166, 171